"*The Come Back Culture* is an important book for leaders of any organization. Designing your experience for employees and for customers is critical for any business to succeed, and this book helps you think about taking both to the next level."

Elizabeth Dixon, speaker; principal leader of service and hospitality, Chick-fil-A

"Service comes from a manual; hospitality comes from the heart. Jason and Jonathan unpack how gracious hospitality and generosity of spirit will lead to powerful, lasting relationships between people and your business."

Kirk Kinsell, former president and CEO, Loews Hotels; former president, Intercontinental Hotels Group (Americas)

"How the customer feels after interacting with your brand is just as important as what you do for the customer. This is the powerful statement Jason and Jonathan make in *The Come Back Culture*, and it's what they help you focus on for your customers. If hospitality is even remotely part of your business, you need to read this book."

Jeanne Bliss, CEO, customerbliss.com; author, *Would You Do That to Your Mother?*

"It's not enough for a customer to have a good experience with your business; they need to remember it. Memorable moments don't just happen. Jason and Jonathan help you create an experience that customers will remember fondly."

Marcus Marshall, vice president of restaurants and bars, Hospitality Ventures Management Group

"Jason and Jonathan help us understand, through their unique perspective, the importance of building a culture that inspires safety, continuity, and appreciation. No matter who your customer is, this book will help you make better long-term, strategic decisions that set you and your organization up for success."

Russ Holland, vice president of real estate, Inspire Brands

"Service is about meeting needs. Hospitality is about the feeling. To create a memorable guest experience, you need both, and Jason and Jonathan are the perfect people to help you do that."

Chris Meaders, mission coach, Maple Street Biscuit Company

"When you have loyal customers, you can have a healthy and profitable business. *The Come Back Culture* is the book that can help make that happen."

Lance Martin, director of business development, EMPWR Solar

"*The Come Back Culture* guides readers through designing intentional experiences that infuse customer service with the heart of hospitality, resulting in an environment where guests feel safe, valued, and cared for. It takes the often ambiguous or elusive nature of hospitality and makes it digestible and applicable. Because experiencing hospitality is different for everyone, it can often feel like aiming at a moving target. However, Jason and Jonathan offer easy-to-understand examples that give flesh to the conceptual principles required in creating a culture of hospitality that leaves guests excited to come back for more."

Josh Kelly, hospitality operations manager,
Roam Innovative Workplace

"Jason and Jonathan do an excellent job of dissecting the guest-experience interactions between everyone involved—guests, team members, and organizational leadership. If you are looking to empower your team to create meaningful moments with guests, this book provides you with tactical ways to get started."

Raegan Thorp, owner of Raegan Thorp
Real Estate Group, Keller Williams

"Jason and Jonathan's approach to remapping the customer as more of a guest changes the landscape of how every business should treat their customers in order to foster that internal desire to come back for more. They are masters at building the customer experience. Whether you provide a physical product or a service for your guest, this book is a must-read to learn Jason and Jonathan's ten principles to master a winning culture."

Andy Jabaley, agent/owner, State Farm Insurance

"Loyalty in business is primarily based on how someone makes you feel. *The Come Back Culture* demonstrates proven strategies to surprise and delight your guests and keep them coming back. Jason and Jonathan expertly show that having a playbook with tasks to serve your guests is important, but more so is having your team execute the intention of those tasks. This connection will create a higher-level customer experience. Every business owner needs to read this eye-opening book to learn the simple and meaningful details that will create raving fans and set your business apart from the competition."

Maday Martinez de Osaba, head of global sales enablement, Scan One; author, *Ocean of Stars and Dreams*

"In today's business economy, caring for the customer matters more than ever before. This book lays out how any business can intentionally create a culture where customers not only come back but invite others to come with them."

Sonia Postema, chief people officer, HC Brands

"A delighted customer is a loyal customer, and a loyal customer is repeat income. Jason and Jonathan have created the ultimate guide to help you delight customers and keep them coming back time and again."

Ben Thorpe, store manager, Discount Tire

THE
COME
BACK
CULTURE

THE
COME
BACK
CULTURE

10 BUSINESS PRACTICES
THAT CREATE LIFELONG CUSTOMERS

JASON YOUNG *and*
JONATHAN MALM

BakerBooks

a division of Baker Publishing Group
Grand Rapids, Michigan

Published by Baker Books
a division of Baker Publishing Group
PO Box 6287, Grand Rapids, MI 49516-6287
www.bakerbooks.com

Printed in the United States of America

Library of Congress Cataloging-in-Publication Data
Names: Young, Jason, 1978– author. | Malm, Jonathan, author.
Title: The come back culture : 10 business practices that create lifelong customers / Jason Young and Jonathan Malm.
Description: Grand Rapids, MI : Baker Books, a division of Baker Publishing Group, [2022]
Identifiers: LCCN 2021041030 | ISBN 9781540901972 (cloth) | ISBN 9781493436163 (ebook)
Subjects: LCSH: Relationship marketing. | Customer relations.
Classification: LCC HF5415.55 .Y68 2022 | DDC 658.8/12—dc23
LC record available at https://lccn.loc.gov/2021041030

Scripture quotations are from the *Holy Bible*, New Living Translation, copyright © 1996, 2004, 2007, 2013, 2015 by Tyndale House Foundation. Used by permission of Tyndale House Publishers, Inc., Carol Stream, Illinois 60188. All rights reserved.

Portions of this text have been taken from *The Come Back Effect* by Jason Young and Jonathan Malm, published by Baker Books, 2018. Used by permission of Baker Books, a division of Baker Publishing Group.

The authors are represented by the literary agency of The Blythe Daniel Agency, Inc.

Baker Publishing Group publications use paper produced from sustainable forestry practices and post-consumer waste whenever possible.

22   23   24   25   26   27   28   7   6   5   4   3   2   1

To Steve Warnstrom,
for encouraging us to write this book.
As a Chick-fil-A owner/operator, you have used the ideas
in this book to help you, your team, and your guests.
You are a leader worth following.

CONTENTS

FOREWORD

When Jason and Jonathan asked me to write the foreword for *The Come Back Culture*, I was excited to be part of the project. I believe that getting the customer to come back is one of the most important parts of any business, and I know it takes a relentless commitment to excellence to make that happen.

Years ago, as I began to build the processes that would create the culture of the Ritz-Carlton Hotel Company, I wanted to create the most excellent hotel company in the world. I invited people to join me in that vision; I knew I would need leaders who wanted to create something beautiful. This approach allowed our team and brand to win the hearts of guests around the world. I was fortunate enough, even as a young boy in Europe, to work under world-class leaders in the hotel industry for many years before earning leadership roles where I brought to life many of the high standards I was taught.

Yes, I work in the hotel business, but it doesn't matter what business you work in. The customer's expectations are the same no matter the product. They expect the product or service to be without defects, delivered in a timely manner, and delivered by someone who is nice. Customer loyalty is nothing more than customers trusting you. We build trust by providing consistency with flawless products, timely service, and kind, caring customer interactions.

If you are reading this book, you probably already know why customer loyalty (trust) is important to your company. But in our situation at the Ritz-Carlton Hotel Company, I estimated that our average customer was worth about $200,000 to our company over their lifetime. That's why I empowered our team to spend up to $2,000 at a time to make things right for the customer. I knew that customer loyalty would be so lucrative to our business that it was worth the risk of spending up to $2,000 in a moment to recover a guest or to create a memory they wouldn't forget. Since this was a controversial management decision, I should also mention that it was extremely rare for anyone to spend $2,000. The real benefit was the empowerment our teams felt to own and solve just about any problem distracting our guests from having an incredible experience. And as you'll read in this book, empathy and kindness are often the only things needed to fix a problem for a guest.

Caring for guests and delivering excellence are hard work. They are supposed to be. But there's a big reward. Studies show that 70 percent of the market is willing to pay more for the same product if the service is excellent. That means if you have a competitor that has a product identical to yours, you can get more business than them just by providing better service. You can even charge more for that product and still capture more of the market.

My hope for you as you read this book is that you evaluate your business. Does it provide excellent care for the guest—the customer? Even if your business does this well, I would love to challenge your thinking and behavior to get even better. Your competitive advantage may simply be the excellence and care you intentionally and consistently deliver to each guest.

I am glad you picked up this book. Jason and Jonathan have great experience to guide you. You will love the ideas and nuggets on each page. They value all the factors that create care for a guest, and they have repeatedly proven their work.

When you get to the end of the book, you will see what Jason, Jonathan, and I believe. We are convinced that creating a culture of care for both team members and guests allows everyone to win, and the elements you build into your culture can tell your guests you want them to come back again and again.

Horst Schulze

Cofounder, former president, and COO,
Ritz-Carlton Hotel Company

Expert in residence, Arch + Tower

Author, *Excellence Wins*

ACKNOWLEDGMENTS

Jason would like to thank:

My family, for graciously giving me the time and space to write. I know you have sacrificed more than you will admit. Thank you.

Horst Schulze, for modeling how to care for others while also inspiring and challenging me through conversations focused on guests.

Chris Green, my friend, for not just offering support but putting intentional action behind your words. Seriously, thank you.

Jonathan Malm, my writing partner, for your humility, insights, friendship, and easy-to-work-with nature. Writing is truly enjoyable with you. Many more books are ahead of us.

Blythe Daniel, my literary agent, for using your words and actions to show support and kindness to me and my book ideas.

Rebekah Guzman and the Baker Publishing team, for showing consistent support and energy for this book.

Former and current clients, for trusting me to partner with you to create a culture where employees and customers want to come back again and again.

Jonathan would like to thank:

Jason Young, my writing partner, for being consistently great to work with. I feel like our best ideas come out when we chat, and it's genuinely fun.

Joe Cavazos, my business partner, for your incredible ideas, humble spirit, and friendship.

Rob Thomas, for showing me how fun a company can be to work for and giving me an idea of how I wanted to treat my future employees.

Carolina Malm, for always seeming to understand about how things work and helping me see what you do.

Franco Malm, for being due in April and giving me a deadline so this project didn't stall. I love being your dad.

Rebekah Guzman and the Baker Publishing team, for instantly believing in this project and helping make it happen.

Blythe Daniel, my literary agent, for hearing my thousand book ideas and helping me know which to pursue.

INTRODUCTION

We are drawn to areas where our brains perceive safety. There is a segment of our brain whose whole job is to evaluate whether or not we will survive in a certain environment. Our brains are constantly scanning for danger. And if we ever perceive danger, even small amounts, an amygdala hijack takes place. A part of our brain takes over and tells us to respond to the danger. We either fight, fly, or freeze.

When people encounter your business, do they respond one of those ways?

The Come Back Culture, and the hospitality we'll be talking about in it, is essentially this one thing: making people feel safe and comfortable in your environment. Does your business make people feel welcome? Do the options presented to the customer feel safe? Or are there threats that cause people to distrust your organization?

The threats don't have to be as dramatic as someone standing at the front of your business with a gun strapped to their shoulder. They can be little things that remove an element of comfort, causing the amygdala hijack to happen.

Our culture is largely operating in a trust deficit. People are skeptical of politicians. Of wealth. Of racial issues. Of marketing. Of businesses. Remember when you saw someone wearing a three-piece suit as an authority who was there to help? Remember when you thought you could leave your front door unlocked? Remember when you weren't nervous about trick-or-treating with your kids?

Maybe you don't remember those days, because we've been operating from a trust deficit for so long. We now are skeptical of the business suit, worry about the safety of our kids, and are even worried that our neighbors might be threats.

So when a company can create a sense of trust and safety for you, you're much more likely to return. You're likely to keep coming back because the limbic system—the emotional response that kicks in before you can rationalize something—tells you that you're safe there.

As we dive into *The Come Back Culture*, we'll talk about this idea of feelings. We'll talk about how to create an organization that makes people feel safe and welcome. And we'll talk about building a team that inspires trust in your customers.

We'll use the term *guest* in lieu of *customer* quite a bit, partially because we want you to start thinking of your customer as someone you host. They're coming into your figurative home, and it's your responsibility to make them feel comfortable and safe. Whether they're a first-time customer or have been frequenting your business for years, this idea of safety is important.

Throughout the book we'll share personal stories to help illustrate the following principles:

1. Focus on Feeling as Much as Function
2. Create a Culture, Not a Job Title
3. Know the Guest
4. Be Fully Present
5. Think Scene by Scene
6. Recover Quickly
7. Observe Details, Because Everything Communicates
8. Reject "Just Okay"
9. Choose Values over Policies
10. Build a Hospitable Team

To keep things clear, we'll make sure you know whose story is whose. But regardless of which stories belong to which person, we hope you'll start seeing your business environment in the narratives. Your organization can become the type that's magnetic—reaching new guests and creating that sticking point where they ultimately keep coming back for more.

one

Focus on Feeling as Much as Function

JASON

There's only one thing I regret about my wedding. It was the wedding reception.

I got married in my hometown of Atlanta, Georgia. My wife, Stacy, is from Oklahoma City. So obviously we hosted many more of my friends and family than hers at the wedding. And because of that, I was so focused on serving everybody at the reception that I left my wife standing there by herself. I was worried about greeting and hosting everything, and I neglected to enjoy time with her. I let my service overwhelm what the whole event was all about. To this day, that's the one thing Stacy says she wishes I'd done differently—simply been with her at the reception.

I was so focused on the task in front of me that I didn't focus on the most important person.

In many businesses, the guest experiences what Stacy experienced. The service is excellent; not a single task is left incomplete. But the guest feels neglected. They feel *served*, but they don't feel *hospitality*.

Businesses love to talk about serving. Customer service is all about taking care of the needs of the customer. The concept is action-oriented. When you hear "serving a customer," it's all about doing a task.

Have you ever experienced someone new to elite-level customer service? Imagine a new concierge at a fancy hotel trying to remember every task he's supposed to accomplish. The guest just got their questions answered and they're moving to exit the hotel, when suddenly the concierge remembers he's supposed to hold the door for guests. He rushes out from behind his station to get the door, but in the process, he bumps the guest and actually cuts them off from their forward motion.

He's contorting his body trying to hold the door for the guest, who is just standing there feeling awkward and uncomfortable. Sure, the concierge accomplished the task, but he made the customer feel confused and maybe even threatened.

The new concierge technically "served the customer," but through his service he gave the guest a negative emotion. It actually would have been better for him to ignore the task since he missed his window of opportunity.

No matter how over-the-top your service, if it doesn't connect with the emotions of the guest, it isn't hospitality. Hospitality isn't just doing the right things; it's making the customer feel seen, valued, and cared for in the process.

The idea of "feelings" isn't a popular one when it comes to business. Feelings are weird and even a little bit uncomfortable. Apart from the extremes of happy and angry, businesses don't often think through the nuances of what a guest might be feeling when interacting with them. This is especially true of things that feel almost entirely transactional. The truth is, though, that no matter how transactional you get, there will still be feelings involved.

An ATM, for instance, is almost entirely transactional. Yet people experience negative emotions when interacting with it. *Is someone watching over my back to steal my PIN? Will the machine take my card and not give it back? Will it charge me more than I anticipated?* These are big emotions people experience, and that doesn't even take into account the colors of the machine, its cleanliness, the brightness of the screen . . .

If people experience all those feelings when interacting with a machine, how much more do they feel when dealing with an actual person?

JASON

There's a man who works at the Walmart by my house. He perfectly illustrates this idea of service without hospitality. The first time my wife and I encountered him, I had a simple question about the location of an item in the frozen foods section. He cheerily offered to escort me to the item. But once we found it, he didn't leave. He stood a bit too close to me and started talking to me about completely unrelated topics. His gestures felt like an octopus wriggling into my personal space. He didn't simply solve our problem and then ask, "Is there anything else?" He overstayed his welcome in an attempt to be over-the-top friendly.

I told my wife as we walked away, "That dude takes his job for real. And I don't mean that in a good way."

Now when we visit that Walmart, we don't ask this guy for help, because he goes so above and beyond that it actually ruins the experience.

Hospitality is about caring for the emotions of the guest just as much as it is about serving them, if not even more. That means knowing when it's time to go above and beyond the call of duty and when it's time to walk away. Hospitality is about merging the function—the tasks—and the feeling.

Every time a guest has an experience with us, we should honor them enough to deliver the same level of hospitality. But that same level of hospitality might mean responding differently each time, because the experience is about the guest. It's not about making ourselves feel good about the service we provide. It's about making the guest feel good about the hospitality we show.

Many businesses have been "doing" this serving thing for so long that all they worry about is "doing." We need to reimagine what it means to be the guest and what it means to serve them well. This means prioritizing the feelings of the guest over the tasks we perform for them.

JONATHAN

There's a bagel shop by my house that I'm only willing to patronize if I don't have to go inside. If the app isn't working or if I didn't plan ahead to order, I won't order bagels there.

It's not because their bagels are bad. The shop actually makes the bagels my wife and I like the most. But when you go in, there are six people working on bagel orders. You stand at the front of the line, ready to order, and not a single person turns around to acknowledge you. They just feverishly work to fill their orders.

After about two minutes of waiting, if you're lucky, someone will turn around and tell you that they'll be right with you. Two to five minutes more go by, and they're still standing in their assembly line immersed in their tasks.

When you finally get to order, there's another line you stand in to pay. And the whole drama plays out again.

I'm grateful for their tasks, but I just need a little bit of attention. It almost feels like the restaurant is there to serve the bagels, not the customer.

How does this play out in other businesses?

Think about a hotel receptionist. It can be so easy to get caught up in the task of checking in a guest that the receptionist forgets there's a whole story behind why the guest came to their hotel. Maybe it's for a much-needed vacation with their family, or maybe there was a death of a loved one that precipitated the trip, or maybe they just needed to get away from everything. Behind each one of those things is a whole host of feelings.

It's easy for a receptionist to just check the ID, swipe the credit card for incidentals, and hand the guest their room key. The receptionist might talk to the coworker standing next to them because they had a long, exhausting day. Or they could just be focused on the slow computer system or still be thinking about the previous guest who was mean to them.

But hospitality looks different. It acknowledges feelings. As a person approaches the desk, they're experiencing feelings. They might be exhausted, worried about whether the room will be ready, anxious about what they came to this town to do, stressed from the drive in . . . A hotel receptionist who understands this will make subtle changes to their approach. They'll still check in the guest, but they might make the following changes:

- Smile warmly and make eye contact with the guest as they arrive.
- Ask what brings them to town and express empathy for their reason.
- Gauge the speed of the guest. If they're anxious to get to their room, the receptionist will move efficiently. If they want to talk, the receptionist will listen.
- Address the whole traveling party, even kids.
- Make some local suggestions based on answers to earlier questions.
- Walk around the desk to give the guest their keys so it feels more personal and less transactional.
- Invite further questions, taking intentional time to listen and respond.

To sum it all up, the receptionist will realize that the feeling they can give the guest is even more important than the tasks they're performing. They realize that people respond to feeling and that feeling is memorable. Their job is not to give a guest a room key; it's to show hospitality through the act of connecting the guest to the hotel. To be honest, the guest could probably get their own room key; there are many hotel apps that make the check-in process unnecessary. But if the receptionist is able to ease the stress the guest is feeling, then they've performed a valuable function. They have delivered hospitality.

Think of a time you visited a new business. You probably had an impression of the place, and you formed a decision to stay away or visit again.

There are times we can pinpoint why we like a business. But there are other times we aren't sure *why* we liked or disliked a place. It's just something we felt.

There will be people who will return to your business and won't know why. They simply felt good there. And there will be others who won't be coming back. They can't explain to someone who asks why they decided not to return; it was just a feeling.

Feelings are important—often even more important than the function. That's why we must merge the two.

The question to ask when faced with this information is obvious: Do we simply let the tasks go in exchange for the feeling? No. This idea of merging function and feeling is about a perspective shift more than anything. It's not strictly a behavioral change, though this *will* affect our behavior. It's about focusing on the feeling of the task—not simply the task itself.

JONATHAN

There's a coffee shop I visit frequently. I'm a bit of a regular there; they always make my coffee right. I respect that they do their job well. But what made this particular coffee shop my favorite was one simple thing. At some point, each of the baristas moved beyond merely making my coffee to becoming my friend. They began asking my name and asking about my job. In the moment they ask details about me, it feels like they're stepping outside of their role and making a personal connection with me. It's that *feeling* they've injected into my visit.

Don't get me wrong—if they continually messed up my drink order, it wouldn't matter how personal our connection. I probably wouldn't keep going back. The function has to be there. But the merging of the feeling and the function takes the coffee shop from good to excellent.

When the emotion is there, it doesn't feel like someone is just doing their job. It's like they're your friend. It feels like they're rooting for you and doing their job is a way to support you—not just a means to perform a task.

Connecting with the Existing Feeling

Empathy—understanding and acknowledging what the guest is feeling—is one of the most important elements of hospitality. A typical guest experiences various feelings during a visit to a business, and many of them are not good. Understanding those feelings is vital to a successful guest experience. But understanding is not enough. Excellence in hospitality means replacing those negative feelings.

A guest who is visiting a business may already be feeling skeptical, nervous, confused, agitated . . . Maybe the traffic was bad. Maybe they've felt cheated by a similar business in the past. Maybe they feel uneducated about the product you're providing and don't want to make the wrong choice. Maybe the price point is already at the end of their budget and they feel nervous about their ability to pay.

If you remember those possibilities, what you deliver has the opportunity to replace that emotion. You could replace a bad emotion with a positive one.

Imagine a customer visiting a quick-service restaurant. It's lunch hour in a busy urban environment, and the front counter is chaos. There's no queuing system, so people just pile into a clump and wait their turn.

You can probably already guess what the guest is feeling, because we've all been in that situation. They're worried about (1) accidentally cutting in front of someone who got there before them and (2) getting cut in front of. They're feeling rushed, and it's taking longer than they were planning for their lunch hour.

Now imagine the staff at the restaurant doing nothing to bring order to the chaos. They just wait at their registers for the next person to come up and place their order. They're leaving the environment for the guests to figure out. Everyone will still be able to place their order and get their food, but there's very little hospitality happening in that moment. The employees have failed to replace a negative emotion with a positive one.

What if, instead, one of the employees took it upon themselves to keep track of who came in and when, and they directed the traffic. Automatically, it would bring a sense of relief to the guests. Then, to take it further, the employee could address each person who walked in, welcoming them and letting them know they're keeping track of the order of people. They might address the stress of the situation and thank people for their patience, even offering a free size upgrade to people's meals or making a joke that the kitchen staff will be adding extra love to their meals that day. That would be bringing hospitality into the mix.

Then, if the employee wanted to replace the emotions the guests were experiencing, they'd take it a step further. They'd walk through the line in a relaxed manner, matching the pace of the guests, and take some drink orders. They'd give the customers waiting something to occupy themselves with so they would at least feel like they're making progress in their meal. Though a small gesture, this would provide a great sense of hospitality.

The original emotions were stress and worry. The replacement emotions were ease and delight. You can bet the guest would remember that feeling when they thought back on whether they wanted to visit the restaurant again.

The role of hospitality is to protect how the guest feels and to give them the best possible experience.

Becoming a Broker

We're all familiar with the idea of a bodyguard. In fact, you've probably seen a dramatic scene in a movie where a gunshot rings out. The film slows down as the brave bodyguard hurls himself in front of the person he's protecting. His body inches in front of the bullet, which then makes impact. The film speeds up, chaos ensues, and you see the relief on the protected person's face. The bodyguard saved their life by taking the bullet. The brave protector considered the life of his client more important than his own.

While it's not going to be quite so dramatic, that's essentially the role a team member should take for their guest. They are a shield—a bodyguard for the guest. They broker bad experiences so the guest doesn't have them. When a team member sees themselves as a broker:

- The hotel guest doesn't have to feel lost when they can't find the elevator. The receptionist leaves their desk and walks them to the elevator.

- The restaurant guest doesn't have to feel embarrassed when their child spills a large beverage all over the table. The waiter gladly takes that emotion on themselves and cleans it up.

- The gym guest doesn't have to feel embarrassed that they don't know how to use a certain piece of equipment. An employee notices and walks over to give a quick lesson.

Brokering the experience for the guest is about sheltering them from the negative emotion. It's jumping in front of the uncomfortable bullet and absorbing it so the guest doesn't have to experience it.

JASON

Back in the day, I worked at a Honey Baked Ham near my house. I wasn't a manager, but I felt the responsibility for the experience people had when visiting the store.

Now, at holiday times like Easter, Thanksgiving, and Christmas, the lines get pretty long. One particular day, the line was way out the door. I could sense people in the back asking, "How long will this take?" They were agitated because they had to deal with this long line on top of all the other stress they had at Christmastime.

So I took it on myself to address those things. I would stand on the counter (with permission) and communicate with the customers. I even did giveaways. When people got to the counter, I'd say, "Because you've been waiting in line longer than five minutes, I would like to offer you something extra."

Was it embarrassing to stand on the counter and yell out instructions to everyone? Of course! But I wanted to communicate to the people in line that I saw they were there and we were working to take care of them. Nobody told me to do that. Yet I also knew my manager trusted me to provide excellent hospitality in my role, so I felt empowered to do it. And even if I hadn't had authority to give things away, I still could have addressed people in the back of the line and let them know what steps we were taking to get them through the line as quickly as possible.

Acknowledgment goes a long way toward hospitality. A guest could internally be asking, *How am I doing? Do you see me? Are you there for me?*

What a powerful thing when we can broker the experience for our guests! When we acknowledge what they're feeling and work to protect them from negative emotions, we make a guest feel truly honored.

In fact, you can even use words that address their feelings. It disarms a guest when you say something like:

- "I don't want you to feel lost."
- "You got here at the perfect time!"

We never want to reinforce a guest's insecurities. Instead, we want to reinforce their security. Their comfort. Their confidence. Those emotions are memorable and will stick with the guest long after their visit is over.

What a Guest Should Feel

Each day, ask yourself two questions to get this idea of hospitality stirring in your head.

1. Today, how do you want your guests to feel? Then ask, in the moment, how you can encourage a guest to feel the way you've decided you want them to feel.

2. How do you want your team members to feel today? Understand that the way a team member feels directly affects how they will make the guest feel. You shouldn't expect your team members to take care of a guest if they don't feel cared for by the organization or the team. Put wind in the sails of your team—because that's what they're going to do for the guest.

What do you want your guests to feel? What do you want them *not* to feel? Determine in your heart and with your team how you will get the guest to feel the good feelings and stay away from the bad feelings.

For instance, if you're a mechanic at an auto shop, figure out what you want your customer to feel as they bring their car in. You would explain things well in terms that make sense to a non-mechanical person. You would address the idea that they think you'll take advantage of them or leverage your expertise over their lack of knowledge. You'd work to make them feel confident in bringing their car to you.

Or if you run a car dealership, you'll understand that the customer is expecting to feel worn down and sold to. You might remind them that you don't haggle at your dealership. You would remind them that you don't want to waste their time with the back-and-forth of car sales (and you'd make sure to remove those delays from the process).

As a manager, expose your employees to both the good and the bad feelings so they can know what positive feelings to deliver in order to replace the negative ones. Train your team to become experts on intentionally delivering positive feelings in a manner similar to how bankers are trained to deal with counterfeit money: know the fake exists, but only deal with the real so you know when you see and feel the fake. Similarly, know that negative feelings happen, but show your team what's possible.

Check out the lists below and highlight the positive feelings that stick out to you. Then underline the negative feelings you've experienced in guest services environments.

You want your guests to feel

- confident
- safe
- satisfied
- accepted
- hopeful

- acknowledged
- empowered
- educated
- pleased
- comfortable
- excited
- interested
- valued
- relaxed
- welcomed
- familiar
- included
- refreshed
- challenged
- secure
- in control
- delighted

You don't want your guests to feel

- confused
- unsafe
- skeptical
- cynical
- suspicious
- ignored
- annoyed
- doubtful

- angry
- hurt
- distrustful
- processed
- rushed
- uneasy
- frustrated
- uninitiated
- overwhelmed
- uncomfortable
- out of control
- helpless

Key Points and Takeaways

1. Serving is task oriented; hospitality is feeling oriented. Simply performing tasks is not enough to compel a customer to come back.

2. Hospitality should change the way we perform our tasks. Tasks are important, but it's the intangible feelings we transmit that turn them into moments of hospitality.

3. People could be feeling negative emotions when they arrive at your business (frustration, apprehension, or confusion). Our job in the come back culture is to replace those negative emotions with positive ones.

4. Great hospitality is shielding the guest from negative experiences by throwing ourselves in front of the

situation—like a bodyguard takes a bullet for the one they're protecting.

5. Decide proactively what you want your guests to feel, then look for ways to create environments that will help them experience that.

6. Imagine if your business was the least-hurried moment of your guest's week. That could be the ultimate thing to compel them to return.

two

Create a Culture,
Not a Job Title

Culture. What a buzzword! You hear it everywhere in the business world. But what does it even mean? What is a culture, and what does it mean when you apply it to guest services?

Simply put, *culture* is the identity of a people group. It's who they are. It encompasses their art, food, entertainment, traditions, and so on. When you add all those things together, you get a group's culture.

JONATHAN

I grew up in the mountains of Central America. My parents were humanitarian workers in the small country of Guatemala. We lived near the city, but most of our work happened in tiny villages that we traversed dirt roads to reach. My parents, along with us three kids, would take our blue-and-silver Suburban over bumpy roads to work in

41

orphanages and feeding centers in these impoverished villages. Part of this ministry also involved going into families' homes and visiting with them—getting to know them and understanding their culture.

On our first visit to one of these homes, we noticed something interesting. When we entered the small cinder-block home with poor ventilation and dirt for flooring, we saw the man of the house fish in his pocket for a few *quetzales* (Guatemalan currency) and call his son over. The young child took the money from his dad and then ran barefoot across the village to a local *tienda* (a small refreshment kiosk). A few minutes into our conversation, the boy returned with some ice-cold bottles of Coca-Cola—one for each of us. We tried to insist that we weren't thirsty and that they didn't need to do this for us. We knew it was probably a financial stretch to provide five bottles of Coke for our family. But they insisted, and we eventually gave in.

We noticed this at every subsequent house we visited. Each time, the parents sent one of their children to buy their honored guests a Coke. We found out through our years of ministry that this is what they do in these Guatemalan villages. It was their way of welcoming guests into their home. It had become part of their identity. It was their culture.

Hospitality can't just be a job title at your business. It's not just the team's job to provide hospitality to new guests. Instead, it needs to be a cultural element of your organization—a shared value. These Guatemalan families didn't have to think about what they would do when a guest visited them. It was already ingrained in the family that you send your kid running to the nearest *tienda* to buy a Coca-Cola for your guest.

When something becomes part of the culture in your organization, expectations are clear. It's seen in everything and everyone. There's no discussion or debate. There's no negotiation. Everyone knows what to do, and they do it consistently.

Also, when something becomes part of the culture, it's portable and memorable. That "Coca-Cola for a guest" tradition in Guatemala was the same in each house. Whether the family lived in a small house or in a large house, they still did it. Whether the guest was Guatemalan or glow-in-the-dark white like the Malm family . . . Something that's cultural is easy to pass along and easy to act on. It's valued from generation to generation—old to young.

You can say something is cultural in your organization, but if it isn't a shared value that's clear, portable, and memorable, it's not really the culture.

JASON

COVID-19 altered hospitality for a lot of places. My family and I were actually surprised when we found it affected one of our favorite places in the whole world: Disney World.

My wife, kids, and I went to Disney in 2021. We were excited because we hadn't been able to go in a while due to the pandemic, and we always felt amazing when we went to Disney. The cast members (that's what they call employees) did everything they were supposed to do, but we left feeling like it just wasn't the Disney we knew and loved. The spirit of hospitality wasn't present.

Many of the cast members were more irritable. They

lacked patience toward guests. Sure, they accomplished tasks, but it wasn't as hospitality focused.

Now, that was understandable. One of Disney's primary goals during the pandemic was to keep the parks open by making them as safe as possible. Safety is always their number-one goal, and you could sense that even more. Safety actually became the biggest goal for the organization, even over the magic, and it perfectly represents what happens when the culture shifts.

Disney's culture is one of hospitality and making the guest feel like the most important part of the process, but in the stress of the urgent, that culture got lost.

You see, your business has a culture, whether you know it or not. And that culture might not be what you hope it is. Your culture is how your people—owners, managers, employees, and even customers—*actually* behave.

An organization can do all the right things. They can check off all the boxes, but if those things aren't actually part of the culture, they feel phony. It has a "your call is important to us; please stay on the line" feel, like the response you get when you call a customer service number. The words don't matter because the heart isn't there. Culture is what makes a response feel genuine instead of robotic.

When guest services becomes part of the culture of your organization, you'll notice it has these three elements:

1. It's a pervasive identity.
2. It's valued from the top down.
3. It's valued with resources.

Let's take the rest of the chapter to look at these three things more in-depth. Examine your own business and see if hospitality is merely a department or a culture.

Culture Is a Pervasive Identity

JASON

Anthony works in events. A woman who attended an event at our organization couldn't find her car. She kept walking in one door and out the other. She was becoming visibly frustrated looking for her vehicle—and dealing with our multiple levels of parking. She was frustrated with herself for not remembering where she parked. Anthony noticed her.

Anthony was done with his responsibilities. He was just about to leave to go home and be with his family. But instead of handing off the responsibility to another team member, he spent the next half hour asking some key questions to help the woman find her vehicle. He was off duty. He had other places to be, but he chose to stay and take care of her. He eventually helped her find her car, and she was so grateful.

I met with Anthony the next day to see how the event had gone, and he relayed this story to me. I praised him and asked him why he would do something like that. His response demonstrated that hospitality was cultural for him—that he gets it. He said, "Because that's what we do for people." He explained that this attitude is what he's seen modeled from management. "Do for one what you wish you could do for everyone" comes from every conversation from the team. It's who we are as an organization.

Anthony identified with our cultural value of serving people well. Then he owned that identity. He saw something that was wrong and corrected it, even though it was no longer his responsibility. He understood that even though you aren't "on the clock," time doesn't limit when you provide hospitality.

When hospitality becomes a cultural value instead of just a department, it becomes part of people's identity. It becomes so ingrained in each member of the organization that they're even willing to call out others when they don't model the correct behavior.

How do you know when a culture of hospitality has pervaded your organization? You'll see it go beyond the confines of your building or events and get into people's everyday lives. Some of the best service organizations witness this phenomenon.

For instance, it's well known that Chick-fil-A trains their employees to respond with "my pleasure" when somebody thanks them. This response has become part of the culture of Chick-fil-A—so much so, in fact, that you'll hear employees say it when they aren't even working. You can spot someone who has worked at Chick-fil-A when you hear that response. It's a telltale sign.

That phrase is an indication that hospitality has become part of the culture of that organization—when the behaviors and values transcend the confines of the job. Hospitality is not just a program or a department. It's an attitude that works its way into people's everyday lives. It begins to influence how they respond to others—at work, at home, in social situations, even on vacation.

A culture that strongly values hospitality begins when people in your organization react consistently to your guests. Then they start responding to their colleagues the same way. Then to salespeople or restaurant employees. Ultimately hospitality works its way into every circle of their everyday lives. It ceases to be something they do. Instead it becomes something they feel—empathy bleeds into every interaction they have.

Culture Is Valued from the Top Down

JONATHAN

I meet with midlevel leaders over coffee often. As we dive into the conversation, I frequently hear familiar stories. These people feel like cogs in the machine of their business. They feel like they only have value based on their last fifty-hour work week, causing them to feel more like a transaction than a valued individual.

This manifests itself in discouragement and burnout. Their leadership asks for long hours and under-resources the team. Consequently, that's how they begin treating the people they manage. They snub team members who take a few weeks off for a family vacation. Or they serve guests well but leave their employees feeling ragged and underappreciated. Thus, that's how their employees begin treating guests. The poor treatment was all under the guise of "serving," but it was really impersonal and transactional. It started from the top.

On the other hand, I occasionally meet with leaders who are in healthy environments. Of course the culture isn't perfect—no team is—but there's a sense that the leadership wants to empower the team. They support their team with resources. They're kind and caring. And they recognize the team's contributions and look for ways to give back to the team. That bleeds down into the employees and then into how the employees treat guests.

A strong hospitality culture comes from the top down. It isn't enough to tell your team to treat guests with empathy. You must model it for them. St. Anthony of Padua said, "Actions speak louder than words; let your words teach and your actions speak."[1] It's important that you use words to cast vision for your organization's culture. But your actions will give power to those words. Actions transform functions into culture.

When hospitality is valued from the top down, there are other benefits to your business. A healthy culture can have the power to

- attract more talent to your organization
- deepen engagement and motivation of your team
- increase retention of volunteers and team members
- raise worker satisfaction and performance levels[2]

This doesn't just affect those who deal directly on the front line with the guest. This sort of hospitality culture permeates the whole organization in positive ways. It becomes the organization's culture.

If you're a leader in your organization, you can influence culture through many things. You can make policies, bring in new employees who model proper behavior, set vision or mission statements, and improve the physical environment of the organization. Those are all good, and they should be part of your leadership. But ultimately, the strongest way to influence culture is through leadership, trust, and treating team members with empathy.

Pouring a little water over a pyramid might get a bit of the lower portions wet. But if you want to saturate the pyramid, you have to completely drench the top so the trickle can reach every area beneath. As a leader, you're the apex of the pyramid. You have to make sure you model your organization's culture enough that there's plenty to reach those below you.

Culture Is Valued with Resources

JONATHAN

My wife loves fitness. She's one of those CrossFit fanatics. Her idea of a good workout is bloody blisters on her hands and a dull ache in her lower back.

I value working out, but I value it in the sense that I think it's a cool thing to do. My idea of working out is going for a light jog when the weather is nice.

I used to tell my wife how much I appreciated and valued her interests. But I didn't want to pay the $160 per month that CrossFit demanded in order for people to join their cult. Yet I was perfectly fine with paying monthly fees for cable, audiobooks, new gadgets, and other toys that were "necessary for my business."

Would you believe my wife wasn't buying it that I valued her interests? She didn't believe I valued her love of CrossFit until we decided together to put money toward it. Until I agreed to put our cash on the table, my words were empty.

―――――――――

Some say to "put your money where your mouth is." President Biden said his dad put it this way: "Don't tell me what you value, show me your budget. I'll tell you what you value."[3] The point is, you don't really value something until you're willing to put your money behind it.

For many businesses, a come back culture is more of an aspirational value than a present value. They would like to create a compelling environment that makes repeat purchases the norm, but they aren't willing to devote the resources necessary to make it happen. The only way an aspirational value becomes a present value is when money backs it up.

The world saw this really well during the COVID-19 pandemic. Some restaurants cut staff to make it, and some actually increased staff to make it—the perfect example being dine-in versus quick-service restaurants. Many dine-in restaurants were cutting hosts, making people wait a bit longer than normal to find their seats. So from the get-go, customers experienced frustration when it came to hospitality. Dine-in restaurants thought the customers' core experience was eating a meal at a table, but there was so much more missing from the experience when they cut key people.

Then you have places like Chick-fil-A that actually closed the inside of their restaurants. Employees who might normally be devoted to cleaning the inside of the restaurant or wandering around the tables were moved outside. Chick-fil-A expedited the outside experience and provided excellent service. And they saw the results by being the best-performing quick-service restaurant in terms of income.

Both types of restaurants cut back on operations, but Chick-fil-A prioritized hospitality. So they won.

Marketers have long known this principle of putting money where they want growth. A business doesn't just start spending money on advertising once they have a bit of excess cash. No, they put money into advertising *in order to* get the extra cash. You have to put money into the areas where you want growth.

Show us your budget items, and we'll show you what your organization truly values. If you want hospitality to stop being just a department in your business—and if you want it to become a strong cultural value—you need to put your resources there. You need to value it with more than just words.

How a Culture of Hospitality Looks in Different Industries

Kitchen Staff at a Restaurant

- The cooks and chefs add special little touches to the plates. They make custom changes so the food feels more individualized.
- The cooks treat each other kindly and smile as they prepare the food.

Housekeeping Staff at a Hotel

- The staff acknowledges the guest walking through the halls—they'll say hello and ask how the guest's day is going.

- They'll add little touches or special things in the room (like those cool swans that they put in the rooms on cruises).
- They might leave a personal note after cleaning the room, wishing the guest a great day.

Appliance Service and Repair Technician

- The technician won't just fix the problem. They'll explain what they're doing as they're working and maybe even give some simple, free tips to help keep the problem from happening again. They certainly won't try to sneak in work that doesn't need to be done.
- The technician will personally call the homeowner when they're on their way to give the exact time they'll arrive.
- The technician will compliment the homeowner for calling them, saying, "It's a good thing you caught this when you did." That reaffirms the homeowner's decision to call the company and empowers them.

Examine your business. Do you see proof of a come back culture? What about in specific departments within your business? What can you do to create a culture of hospitality that compels guests to come back and experience more?

Key Points and Takeaways

1. Hospitality can't be just a job title. It should be an organization-wide, reflexive response.

2. Your business has a culture, but it's not necessarily going to be what you hope. You have to be intentional about creating a culture of hospitality.

3. A culture of hospitality bleeds into your team members' everyday lives. Hospitality can't just be something that happens a few hours a day.

4. When something is part of the culture, it is phrased in terms of "who we are," not "what we do."

5. Hospitality starts with leadership. Hospitality is how leadership treats the staff and how the staff treats the customer.

6. Hospitality isn't a part of the culture until money and resources are devoted to it.

three

Know the Guest

In the international business space, American companies have seen the potential that a massive market like China can bring to their company. So a ton of industries are moving to China to market their products, yet they're discovering it more difficult than they'd thought. A new report suggests that one of the key problems Americans have in marketing their products in China is that they don't understand the culture. Only half of the companies listed in the report even adjusted their marketing strategies to reach Chinese consumers.[1]

So often people in marketing look at things like demographics (age, gender, marital status, stage of life, area of residence, ethnicity). These types of things are easy to get from customer surveys and census data. Unfortunately, companies in China need to have more than just demographic information on their customers to be successful.

We even see this in the United States. A few years ago everyone was trying to reach the elusive Millennial market.

So they created an avatar of every single person born in a certain date range and treated them like a cohesive unit. The same thing is happening with Generation Z. But this type of lumping together based on age demographics misses a huge part of the picture.

There's nothing wrong with knowing demographics. We can get some valuable insights from this type of information. Different ages and different genders tend to behave certain ways. The same is true for those who are affluent or those who are impoverished. But if we want to take our hospitality to the next level, we need to know more. We need to know what the service industry has labeled *psychographic information*.

The term *psychographics* can seem daunting. But quite simply, psychographics are measurements dealing with someone's psychological state. These are things like personality, values, attitudes, interests, and lifestyles.[2]

While demographics might be able to tell you that your customer base is filled with affluent white couples in their forties, you can't rely on believing all wealthy white couples in their forties think and act the same way. For instance, wealthy oil tycoons in Texas think and behave quite differently from wealthy actors in Hollywood. Or wealthy professionals in Miami. Or wealthy estate owners in Maine. While money might be a unifying factor for these four groups, lumping them all in the same category would yield some ineffective results.

When you don't know your guest inside and out, you risk faux pas when dealing with them. In 2014, Apple committed this type of psychographic faux pas when they announced their newest iPhone release. In an attempt to create buzz and show appreciation to their iTunes users, they automatically gave every user U2's newest album release. For some users, that meant it automatically downloaded to their phone or their computer. It seemed like a good idea. U2 is about as big as a band can get—they're internationally famous and even revered. But some users responded to the event with outrage. A social media storm ensued, with people complaining that their devices were running out of space or that their security had been violated.

Apple failed to consider the values, attitudes, and interests of their iTunes users. They assumed they knew the user, but they didn't take the time to truly understand them. Apple and U2's generous gesture was taken as a curse.

This is the risk we run when we don't know the guests who grace our parking lots and storefronts, tables and rooms. What's intended as a gesture of kindness and welcome can be an affront to the guest.

Businesses that get this "know the guest" practice right learn as much as possible about their guest. They'll know details like what magazines they read, what television shows they watch, and even where they get their news. This is a deeper level of understanding, but it translates to a come back culture.

When you intentionally understand the who and let that inform your why, you inevitably create a more remarkable and targeted experience of hospitality.

How Do You Get This Information?

Companies like Zappos and Amazon rely on psychographic data as if it were a life preserver in a stormy ocean. They rely on consultants and intense market research to get this information because these companies are highly competitive.

One experience that doesn't match a user's values and attitudes can send them running to the competitor. Fortunately for smaller businesses, it doesn't take quite as much to get this type of information. You don't need to rely on market research and consultants to get the information you need (though it certainly wouldn't hurt).

JASON

I work with many organizations, and surveys are an important part of what we do. We do them biannually, asking questions like:

"Based on your overall experience, how was it?"
"Would you come back?"
"Would you bring someone with you?"

But more simply than that, we take a page out of the Disney playbook when it comes to obtaining psychographic data. We create multiple listening posts—designated eavesdroppers, if you will—throughout the organization, and then we ask them, "What did you hear today?"

I frequently ask this, so my team members have begun listening for those types of things. They say, "We kept hearing about the coffee," or "People were frustrated with the temperature in the building," or "Guests inquired about how we choose the music in the building." This type of information is invaluable in the way that it informs specific psychographic variables. You discover people's values very quickly when you see what areas of frustration arise in your guest services protocols.

It's easy to forget that you have your own market analysts in the form of your team members. Don't overlook this fact. Talk with people who are interacting with those you're trying to reach. Your fellow team members will give you the insights and information you need in order to know your guest. It's as simple as priming employees to listen for specific feedback or even ask specific questions of customers.

These are some of the questions you can ask your team members and guests:

- **What's right?** What functioned properly and made sense for the guest?
- **What's wrong?** Where did we miss the mark?
- **What's missing?** Was the guest expecting something that we didn't anticipate? Follow-up? Signage?
- **What's confusing?** What questions do we consistently answer? What questions take the longest to answer?[3]

Find ways to ask these questions each week or after an event. Begin to collect all this data. As a team, create a profile of your guest so you can begin crafting your hospitality experience to accommodate their psychographic variables.

What Do You Do with Conflicting Data?

JONATHAN

For one of my companies, we set up a Facebook group to get instant information from our customers. We ask questions that help us determine changes to products and pricing and even release bonus content in the group. It's an invaluable tool for connecting with our customer base.

We've opened up the lines of communication so much that our customers frequently make suggestions in the group, even when we don't ask. We have one very vocal customer who is constantly sharing his thoughts on things that would make our company better. For instance, every month or so he begs us to design T-shirts for our company.

I can tell you with near certainty that few of our other customers would buy a T-shirt with our logo on it. It doesn't reflect the values and preferences of our base. We could make a bunch of T-shirts based on this very loud feedback, but it would be a huge waste of time and energy for our team. Then we'd be confused as to why nobody was buying them even though we designed our best shirt and marketed it with all of our energy.

This story is an example of conflicting data. The truth is, there will always be some people who prefer X while others prefer Y. If you put too much stock in either opinion, it's easy to become reactionary. It's easy to flip-flop on a whim based on anecdotal evidence.

When you get the data from your frontline team members, it's important to submit those stories to an overarching understanding of what you know about people. Look for volume, patterns, and impact. If 90 percent of people say the same thing consistently, there's a good chance you need to do something about it. Never react to one story from one guest.

Also look for the why or the motive behind the feedback: "Why do you like this?" or "Why don't you like this?" Often these stories will relate to a single personal experience. It might remind the guest of a good experience they had with an unrelated company. Or they might have a different family background that made certain social taboos acceptable to them.

Never make knee-jerk reactions to stories or single opinions. Always keep the big picture in mind.

What Do You Do with This Information?

JASON

One of the organizations I worked with made breath mints available in the lobby and the restrooms. This was yet another way we could make a guest feel comfortable in the building—fresh breath provides a definite confidence boost.

For a long time we provided those red-and-white peppermints that your grandmother used to carry in her purse. But based on some psychographic data, we learned those didn't really reflect the preferences of our guests, although they didn't verbally say so. Using the data we'd gathered, I changed the type of breath mints we served to a brand-name wintergreen mint.

It was a subtle change, but it reflected a huge difference in the way we welcomed the guest. Previously we went through about five large bags each month of the red-and-white mints. But after making this change, we started going through about seventy-two bags each month. Obviously, wintergreen mints reflected our guests' preferences better.

Now, that's a silly example. But that one small detail tells the guest that we see them and we value them.

Mints might seem like a nitpicky change to make. But there are larger changes to make using this psychographic data. Here are some possibilities:

- An Uber driver might ask the rider if they prefer a quiet or chatty ride. They might even take their cue from which seat the rider chooses.
- A gym that recognizes their clients are health nuts might serve pizza one night a month for fun.
- A real estate agent takes notice of their clients. Are they a young married couple buying their first house? Or is this their third or fourth house purchase? The agent will gauge their advice so it isn't too vague for the newbies or too heavy-handed for the seasoned pros.
- A liquor store in a college town might realize a lot of their customers aren't familiar with alcoholic beverages, so they have recipes for cocktails and even suggest brands to use that make the buying experience less foreign to their new customers.
- A retirement community in twenty years might realize they're getting Millennials in their building. They'll start playing *The Office* on repeat in the common rooms. They'll have charcuterie Wednesdays. They'll have selfie rooms and video game stations where people can play *Halo* together.

Some of those are real examples. Some of them are ideas. And some might even seem a bit outlandish. But they represent organizations knowing their customers and crafting an experience for them.

Another way you can know your guest is by staffing according to who they are. Imagine a large clothing or department store, for instance, that has a section for teenagers. What type of person should the store place in that section to help the guest? Most likely it would be a younger woman who dresses and behaves in a way that many teenagers aspire to. There would be an instant level of trust that the clothes the guest buys from this individual would meet their needs. The primary concern of a teenager buying clothes is, "Will this make me look cool?" So placing someone in that department who can help the guest answer that question and affirm them is a hospitable way of knowing them.

Subconsciously, the guest wants to see

- someone like them when they enter the door
- someone with an empathetic response because they connect with a particular life stage (parent, student, retired)
- someone displaying similar behavioral elements

Behavioral elements are things that characterize how a guest behaves in public and how they expect to be treated. These are different depending on location and psychographic segments. For instance, your parents or your children might have behavioral elements completely unique from you.

These are some of the main behavioral elements of guests:

- *Emotional and social distance.* They may not be ready to get too friendly and too detailed about their lives when you first meet them. They might not even be comfortable with a handshake.

- *Distrust of the business.* Maybe in the past they've felt pressured to buy something they didn't need. They might assume the only thing your organization cares about is the money in their wallet.
- *Desire to be in control.* They may need to initiate contact, and you should allow them that privilege. Businesses normally prefer to initiate, so this may feel out of the norm. Serve the environment and the person, but go slow and let the guest be in control.
- *Expecting people to be responsive.* They may want your team to be timely and helpful and to embrace responsibility throughout the process.

If you're a leader, train and staff your team using this type of psychographic information. Let your team know what to expect. Introduce them to what guests might be like, and teach them to empathize with what guests might experience during a visit. Properly using psychographic information can make a large business feel small in the best ways, and a small business feel large in the best ways.

Imagine this scenario: You order an appliance from a big-box store. You schedule a delivery time on the store's website, then an individual calls you. They confirm with you that the appliance will be delivered on that date, then they give you a personal line to contact them at. (You don't have to go through a number tree to get to someone who will then have to look you up.) A week before the appliance is delivered, the person calls you again to confirm the date. They ask if you need to reschedule or if there's any information they need in order to deliver the appliance successfully. They also ask if you have any questions. That information is passed on directly to the person doing the delivery so the process feels seamless. Then the morning of the delivery, you receive one last call to confirm the delivery window, with a direct number to call if something changes or more questions come up.

This scenario can make a small business feel large because the system is responsive and not too invasive. It can also make a large business feel small because the contact person got back to you quickly, remembered you, and gave you a personal point of contact.

Getting the Whole Team There

So we've presented the goal, but how do you get there with your team?

You don't need to use the term *psychographics*. But your team should create an outline of what your typical guest looks like. Even though a wide range of people will interact with your business, you'll notice a trend toward a certain type of person. Create a sheet that outlines the values, preferences, and life stage of that person. Get specific—down to things like shows they watch, magazines they read, and life goals they have. (Check out the appendix for an example of a psychographics sheet.) Narrow down the focus of your hospitality team by introducing them to the guest. Tell them, "This is the person we have coming through our door. How should we respond to them?"

A great way to start integrating a welcoming atmosphere for this type of guest is through hiring new people to become part of the team. Hire people who reflect the guest. Look for people with the right body language, a responsive nature, and even a style that reflects your target guest's psychographic state. Obviously there are hiring laws that prevent discriminating based on demographic data, but the good news is you aren't as concerned with demographic data as you are with psychographic data. There are people from every demographic layer who can match your hiring standards.

If you're the leader of the team, train them to start empathizing with the guest. Note that a new approach can take a long time for them to get right. Be patient with this. Listen and continue to reinforce the vision and the why behind this new approach. For good or for bad, so much of guest services is driven by emotion. So give your team an emotional landscape they can relate to.

Start by using the word *imagine*:

- Imagine if a guest saw someone who acted and thought like they do in the way you responded to them.
- Imagine if a guest felt comfortable in your organization, even though they've harbored distrust for businesses and salespeople.
- Imagine if a guest felt in control of the situation, even when they've been completely out of control the rest of the day.

Once your team has imagined the scenario, close with some questions: "What if we could make a guest feel like that? What is it going to take for us to do that?" Guide them to the appropriate answers.

Continue to lead your team with vision as they adjust to the new approach to knowing the guest. Change doesn't have to be sudden. In fact, your best opportunity to get your team members to know your guest will be through small changes over a period of time. Imagine if, each week, you make small changes to better reach your guest. You make one small tweak, then you evaluate it. The next week, you make another small tweak, then evaluate. Over a year's time, that's fifty-two small changes. While each change might not have been revolutionary, the sum of all those changes at the end of the year would be massive. This helps keep you from having knee-jerk reactions, and it helps bring the rest of the team along for the journey.

The Ritz-Carlton hotel chain takes this approach when it comes to creating a team culture. All of their locations, no matter what country they're in, do a training moment each week. The teams go through all twenty-four of their values, one per week, and drill it into their staff members. Once they work their way through all twenty-four, they go back to the beginning.

As changes happen, some of your current team might become displeased or frustrated with the new system. Give them time. But if a team member simply isn't getting on board, you should never sacrifice the comfort of a guest for the preferences of a staff member. In other words, there may come a point where you need to fire them.

Firing is not a bad thing. For some people, getting fired is the best thing that can happen to them. It can set them up to learn how to approach their job better in their next employment situation, and it can help them find the position that's best suited for them. Don't be afraid to let go of people who aren't getting it.

At the end of the day, you are creating remarkable hospitality for your guest. An inflexible team member throws a monkey wrench into the whole thing. Don't allow that to happen. Do all you can, but don't be afraid to lose a team member. Protect the guest's experience at all costs.

What about Targeting?

So often in our businesses, we think we're designing an experience for a guest, but we're really designing it for ourselves. We're designing it for a customer who thinks and behaves exactly like we do. Or worse, we are trying to create an experience for everyone, which means we create an experience for no one.

Jewelry stores understand this concept. Even though we could say nearly all jewelry stores have the same types of things, some have branded themselves engagement ring stores, some have branded themselves diamond stores, and some have branded themselves less expensive or more expensive.

These stores realize that they could try to reach everyone, but they're far more effective whenever they try to reach a certain person. Think specifically about those that brand themselves engagement ring stores. They target the person who will ask their significant other to marry them. So they aren't necessarily marketing to the wearer of the ring; they're marketing to the person who will buy it for the wearer. Thus, their ads are typically geared toward making the person proposing the hero. When that person gets an enamored smile from their significant other, the store is reinforcing that they have the right type of jewelry the customer needs. They're excluding a huge number of people from their ads, but they're doing so to be more effective in their knowledge of the guest.

When you create an avatar of a person using psychographic data, you leave people out. The purpose isn't to be exclusive but instead to make it easier to help the right person find the right business quickly. The periphery of your target audience won't always become loyal customers. But your target will. And you create a remarkable experience for those guests when they engage with your business.

Know the guest, and the guest will want to know you. Remember that how you feel about a guest coming in will be reflected in how they feel about you going out. When you know the guest and they feel it, they'll feel valued—you'll have a come back culture.

Key Points and Takeaways

1. Creating a come back culture starts with knowing more about the guest than just census data. You should know the values, attitudes, and interests of your guest.

2. You can get to know your guest better by asking, (a) "What's right?" (b) "What's wrong?" (c) "What's missing?" and (d) "What's confusing?"

3. When it comes to relating to and knowing the guest, one or two stories from your guests shouldn't cause you to change everything you do as a business. Don't make knee-jerk reactions; instead, look for overall trends to indicate what changes you should make.

4. Respond to your guest, but don't be invasive. Knowing your guest's persona well allows them to be

anonymous when they want while still making the experience feel personal.

5. Fifty-two small changes over the course of a year is more manageable than two or three big changes. Your team will respond best to small tweaks made over time in regards to knowing and relating to the guest.

6. In your community, some people will relate better to your organization than other people will. Having a target audience is simply acknowledging that and helps you reach those people.

four

Be Fully Present

JONATHAN

Recently I was working from a local coffee shop that was about half an hour away from my house. I'd finished the workday early—before rush-hour traffic hit—and got in my car to head home. About thirty minutes after I closed the door to my car, I pulled into my parking spot at the apartment complex and turned off the engine. It's like I emerged from an unconscious state as I realized I had no idea how I'd gotten home.

I couldn't remember what route I took. I couldn't remember if I'd experienced road rage along the journey. I didn't even know what music was playing while I navigated the city streets. Throughout the whole journey, I was so lost in my own thoughts that I didn't process any external stimuli. I was completely inside my own head.

Surely you can relate to that experience. We've all been through situations where our internal autopilot kicks in, and we skate through life completely unaware of what we're doing.

It's even easy to do this in our business. When each week looks and feels like more of the same, it's easy for autopilot to kick in inside our heads. We're performing functions and doing our jobs, but our minds are wandering around elsewhere. We aren't in the moment. If we want excellence in hospitality, we can't afford for anyone on our teams to be like this. We have to be fully present in the moment.

If you're familiar with any psychological or Buddhist teachings, you've probably heard of this concept of being "fully present." It's interchangeable with mindfulness, thoughtfulness, being in the moment . . . It's listening. Awareness. Presence.

There's a story told of Buddha that illustrates being "fully present" perfectly:

> One day the Buddha was speaking to a prince who asked him, "What do you and your monks practice every day?"
>
> The Buddha replied, "We sit, we walk and we eat."
>
> The prince said, "We also do these things every day, so how are you different?"
>
> The Buddha responded, "When we sit, we know we are sitting. When we walk, we know we are walking. When we eat, we know we are eating."[1]

Being fully present is simply being aware of what you're doing. It's about knowing why you're doing what you're doing. In Buddhism, this is because awareness is a transcendental state.

For our purposes, though, being fully present has a completely different motivation. In Buddhism, it's about being self-aware. But in a come back culture, being fully present is about being aware of both yourself *and* the guest. It's about being externally focused so you can fully empathize and connect with your guest. It's laying aside yourself and giving the guest your everything.

When you make the intentional choice to be fully present, you are declaring what you value. Will you value the restaurant you'll eat at for lunch? Will you value that text message buzzing in your pocket? Or will you put all those distractions aside and value the guest?

A parent understands this concept. When a big football game or *Dancing with the Stars* is on television and their child is begging for attention, the parent has a choice. They can try to focus on both—attempt to catch their child's antics in between football hikes or dance numbers. Or they can turn off the television and focus all their attention on the child, becoming fully present in that moment.

We all know which of those scenarios is the right response. (Though acting on it is often much more difficult in the moment.) Through the right response, the parent gets a benefit greater than the thrill of entertainment. The connection they have with their child is far greater—at least in the long run—than that TV show (even the Super Bowl).

When we connect with the life of another person, we both get a lift. It's mutually beneficial.

That's what we're talking about in this chapter. A come back culture is more than just blocking and tackling on the field of your business. It's not just coordinating *X*'s and *O*'s in the game plan. It's about human interaction. When you choose to relate with the guest, you create a great experience.

The intentional human element turns a potentially impersonal process—shuffling a person from their car and through the line, getting their money, delivering their product, saying goodbye—into a moment when the guest feels valued and heard.

The Three Fields of Operation

When we talk about being fully present, there are three fields of operation on which we must play the game. Being present in one of these but not the other two will make for a breakdown in a come back culture. And while it's impossible to analyze your presence in these three fields in the moment, being aware of these areas ahead of time can help you be more fully present for the guest.

Mental

When a man has a conversation with his wife, being mentally present is about the thinking element of conversation. As his wife begins talking, he presses Pause on what he's thinking and presses Play on what she's saying. A thoughtful husband thinks through appropriate questions to ask that will foster the conversation. He thinks through answers to her questions.

He doesn't just listen to key words. "I went to the store and the clerk was so mean to me." *Store*, *clerk*, and *mean* might be the key words, which communicate the facts of what happened. But wrapped up in a sentence like that is so much more depth. There are emotions and deeper truths about the wife found in the middle of those key words. She was expecting something different to happen. She felt a deeper pain than just the pain of someone being mean to her. It might have even reminded her of a painful experience as a child when someone treated her unfairly. A thoughtful husband hears more than just the facts. He listens to the story and then listens through it to what his wife is really saying.

That's the start of being mentally "fully present"—stopping your thoughts and fully engaging with the guest. Taking it a step further, though, you should be listening for the deeper question the guest is asking—sometimes even when there's no actual question involved. Instead of answering the question they explicitly ask, take your response to the next level and offer them an answer to what they're really asking but might be afraid to express.

Disney World trains their cast members to do this well. A famous example is drawn from those people who approach a cast member with the question, "What time is the 3:00 parade?" The answer is obvious: 3:00 p.m. But Disney employees hear this question all the time. And they've been trained to realize that people are *actually* saying, "I need to know when I should get to the parade and where I should sit." A well-trained Disney employee will respond with, "There's a great spot to see the parade at _____. If you get there by 2:25, you'll have to sit there waiting for thirty-five minutes, but your kids will love it. They'll get to sit up front and see the characters." You see, the Disney employee answered the verbalized question, but they also answered the *real* question.

JASON

Another example comes from a time I stayed at the Ritz-Carlton in Atlanta, Georgia. I called the night before we were to check out of the hotel, asking, "What time is checkout?" My *real* question was, "Will I have time to do what I want to tomorrow before I have to check out?" Of course, I was afraid to ask that of the front desk employee. Fortunately, they heard my real question and replied, "Is there a certain time you would like to check out?" I told the employee what I wanted to accomplish, and she replied, "Normal checkout is 11:00 a.m. But how about this: We can set your checkout time to 1:00 p.m. That should give plenty of time for you and your family to enjoy yourselves. Would that be helpful?"

━━━━━

Did you notice how, in each of those situations, being fully present meant taking excellence to the next level? That isn't an easy thing to do if you're thinking about your own problems while trying to listen to the guest. Providing excellence like that requires that you press Pause on what you're thinking and fully invest your mental energy into the guest.

Let's set up a typical restaurant scenario to see if we can discover what a real question might sound like from a guest.

A couple comes into the restaurant with a one-year-old who can barely walk. You, the host, offer to seat them at a two-top table and bring them a high chair. The couple insists on a four-top table.

You begrudgingly walk them over to a table near the wall, but they ask to be moved elsewhere. You can't figure out why they're being so difficult, but you oblige because you don't want to make your manager unhappy with you. The couple senses your annoyance, so they're annoyed. The customer experience has been broken, and they might be unlikely to return to your restaurant again.

76

If you were listening to the questions at face value, it does seem like the couple are being difficult guests. But if you were fully present in their situation, you might realize that their toddler is going to want to move around a lot during the meal. Having more chairs available will help them keep their child entertained, ultimately creating a better experience for the other guests in the restaurant.

You might also realize that the first table you escorted the couple to was near a wall that had a shelf with objects they knew their toddler would be attracted to. They didn't want their child to rain down destruction on the restaurant. What you could have realized was that they actually wanted to be great guests, but they just needed help finding a table that would give them and their toddler the best chance of having a peaceful meal.

That's what listening for the real question looks like. That's being fully present mentally. It's thinking deeper than the face value of what the guest is verbalizing and reaching them on a deeper level.

Physical

JONATHAN

Bobby was a friend who was a mechanic. He grew up in a family full of boys, so he was a tough character. He loved people, though. Unfortunately, because of his rough background—growing up in Boston with brothers who loved to fight—he displayed some odd physical characteristics when he spoke with guests at his shop.

Bobby would jut out his chin and look down his nose at the guest as he spoke with them. It gave the impression that he was ready to fight them. When I approached Bobby and told him how that appeared to a guest, he was completely unaware he was doing it. It was unintentional body language that he had learned when he was a child.

It took Bobby many weeks of intentionally being aware of his body language to break himself of the habit. But as he focused on being fully present with the guest—being self-aware in order to make the guest feel more welcomed—he became an even better business owner and better at interacting with guests at his auto shop.

There's natural body language we all display in different circumstances. When we feel threatened, we cross our arms to feel protected, we avoid eye contact, we frown . . . When we're glad to be around someone, we smile, we brighten our eyes, we open our arms in welcoming gestures, we make eye contact . . . Those positive body language elements are all signs to a guest that we are listening and happy to be doing it. And while the guest might not be fully aware of it, their subconscious is taking cues from our body language and informing them whether they're in a safe environment.

Princeton researchers have found that it takes about one hundred milliseconds to register a first impression—as long as it takes a hummingbird to flap its wings.[2] Be aware of body language as you welcome a guest.

Did you know . . .

- when you point your feet toward the guest, you say, "I am interested in what you are saying"?

- when you smile, you say, "I am happy and friendly"?
- when you properly use your hands, you support the words you are saying?
- when you slouch, you say, "I lack confidence or have low energy"?
- when you cross your arms, you say, "I am uninviting or protective"?
- when you look down, you say, "I am uncomfortable or self-conscious"?
- when you listen while making eye contact, you say, "I care about you"?
- when you bite your nails or play with your hair, you say, "I am anxious or uncomfortable"?

Becoming aware of your body language takes time and practice. (You might role-play in front of a mirror or record yourself in a training session.) But becoming more aware of your physical presence will help you not only in hospitality but in every aspect of your relational life.

The physical element of a come back culture is understanding how your body and expressions communicate to the guest—either making them feel welcomed and safe or putting them in an environment of hostility and emotional distance.

Emotional

One of the most powerful words in the English language is *empathy*. It's vital to relationships. And your guests are longing to have someone who will listen to them. Imagine what would happen if you could do that for them in the thirty seconds you interact with them.

Being fully present emotionally means feeling their anxiety when they are lost. It means rejoicing with them when they explain how happy they are to have discovered your business. It means expressing concern for them when they misplaced their keys somewhere on your property (and leaving your post to help find them).

Creating a come back culture involves understanding the emotion of the moment and solving the problem in a manner worthy of that emotion. The empathy should be real. After all, people know when you're faking it.

You've likely experienced this on a phone call with customer service. "I'm sorry you're experiencing this problem. This is just how our company operates." In that interaction, there was no real empathy—the operator was not sorry. They were just reading a script.

Many of us have experienced the positive side of this, though, at a restaurant. "I am so sorry your food was cold when we brought it out. We dropped the ball there; that's unacceptable. I'm going to remove that meal from your ticket. Would you like me to bring you out a fresh plate that will be hot? Or how about dessert?" The person listened. They empathized with the frustration. And they offered solutions that would solve the real problem as well as the frustration.

Another element of empathy is understanding the negative feelings your guest experiences in every other area of their life and giving them a break from it. Life is hurried. Imagine if you could create the one unhurried moment in their week—letting them set the pace for their visit. That would ignite a desire for them to come back and engage with your business again. Or perhaps throughout most of their week, they feel ignored and unvalued. If you could listen and value your guest, it would offer them a break from what they normally experience. Your actions and your words could say, "I see you, I hear you, and I value you."

That's hospitality mixed with empathy. That's the emotional field of operation in a come back culture.

What the Guest Hears

When you are not fully present with the guest, you're saying to them:

- "You are not important."
- "You are more of a task to be handled than a person to care about."
- "You will receive more robotic responses from me than personal ones."

Inversely, when you *are* fully present with the guest in these three fields, they hear:

- **"I recognize you.** You are not invisible to me. I intentionally choose not to look past you but to care enough to look 'in' you. I acknowledge that you might not want to be seen. However, I will be intuitive enough to sense that and respond."

  Not everyone wants to be treated the same. And being fully present allows you to realize the individuality of a guest and respond in a way that's meaningful to them—whether with a handshake or a nod and a smile.

- **"I am listening to you.** I am choosing to actively listen, which means I restate what you are saying to ensure I listened correctly and so you will know you were heard and I 'got' you.'"

    Hearing someone is not the same as listening to someone. When you listen, you listen to more than words—you listen to their feelings, their body language, and what they are *not* saying. This allows you to hear the questions they are really asking and respond in a way that's meaningful and appropriate.

- **"I want to validate you.** I will normalize the way you are feeling. What you are feeling is common. I don't want you to feel alone in this."

    Being in a new store or restaurant or hotel can be a scary thing. *You* know it's not a high-pressure sales environment, but the guest doesn't. When you acknowledge the fear and anxiety your guest may be experiencing, you allow them to relax a little. You acknowledge what they're feeling and assure them that your business is a safe and comfortable place.

- **"I appreciate you.** I realize you are placing trust in our business. You trust us to take care of your children or to invest in your life with our music, words, and care. I don't take this responsibility lightly."

    Airlines do this when they say, "We know you have a lot of choices when flying. We appreciate you choosing ____ Airlines." It's a simple gesture, but it still expresses a lot.

- **"I am giving you my undivided attention.** My posture is toward you. I am looking at you. I am not preoccupied with anything pertaining to me. Distractions lose. You win. You are my priority."

Put your cell phone away. Delay your chat with your coworker. Focus 100 percent on the guest. After all, the way you feel about a guest coming in will be directly reflected in how they feel about you when they leave.

Practical Ways to Be Fully Present

We've talked about the importance of being fully present. But what does that actually look like? What are some practical ways you can be fully present or ways you can train your team to do this?

1. Watch your body language.

Do a quick full-body scan as you begin your conversation with a guest. *How is my head positioned? Am I making eye contact? Am I smiling?*

Then work your way down. *Are my arms folded or open? Do I have my hands in my pockets? Am I gesturing appropriately? Are my feet angled toward the guest? Am I standing too close? Too far away?*

Once you've performed the body scan, focus all your attention back on the guest.

2. Intermittently repeat back what you are hearing your guest say.

Repeating back what you hear your guest saying might feel silly. But it does two things: First, it helps you verify that you're hearing a guest's concerns and questions accurately.

Sometimes what we hear isn't actually what's being said. Second, it assures your guest that you are listening to them. A guest wants to be heard and understood.

Repetition might look like this: "I hear you saying your child needs his hair cut just with scissors. So you're wanting it to stay long on the sides?" And the next time the guest comes in, you might repeat that question to reaffirm that you were listening and understood them.

3. Be emotionally intelligent.

Emotional intelligence is about understanding the social setting and matching your actions and posture to it. Is the business a casual environment or a formal environment? Is your posture appropriate for such an environment?

What are the guests like? Are your actions appropriate for making these types of guests feel welcomed?

How's the pace of the setting? Are people trying to get their needs met and then leave? Are they hanging around longer?

Emotional intelligence also includes being self-aware. Do you get distracted easily? Are you tired today? Are you anxious about something?

Manage your response to the social setting and to internal obstacles. Continually make adjustments.

4. Understand your role in the big picture.

When you encounter a guest, it's important to realize that they don't know your role. They don't know every responsibility you have; they just know your job is to meet their needs. They aren't aware that their unexpected question might throw the rest of your role all out of whack.

Imagine, for instance, that you're an usher at a live performance. Part of your role is to help guests find their seats, but you perform many other tasks. You check to make sure people are authorized to sit where they are, you reduce distractions, you monitor food coming in so spills don't ruin the show, and you make sure the performers aren't being distracted. Really, your role in the whole scheme of things is to make guests and performers feel confident so they can have the best experience.

True, the show might go on just fine without your involvement. People *could* find their own seats, or the crowd could help discourage distractions. But if you weren't there, fully present, doing your role, your absence would be felt. Understand that your role in the big picture is more than just the tiny tasks you need to accomplish.

5. Personalize the experience.

Pay attention to the guest. Quite simply, that means involving the person, responding to them, and empathizing with what they're feeling—what's important to them. This is about personalizing the experience.

Don't treat every guest the same way. Look for ways you can personalize your welcome. Take cues from their children or spouse, the clothes they're wearing, or the way they walk. Each person walking through the doors of your business is an individual with unique values, dreams, and goals in life. Look for their individuality and customize the guest experience for them.

6. Accomplish your tasks early.

Prepare what you can ahead of time. The less you have to worry about when the guest arrives, the better. If you're doing tasks you anticipated and could have accomplished before the guest arrived, you won't be able to be fully present for them. When you're unhurried, you can more easily be undistracted. You can focus all of your attention—mental, physical, and emotional—on the guest.

Imagine your business being the one place where a guest feels truly heard. The one place in their life that feels unhurried and peaceful. You have the opportunity to offer empathy and comfort in a world filled with chaos.

Something amazing happens when you're fully present for your guests.

Key Points and Takeaways

1. Great personal hospitality requires being fully present—nothing distracting you from fully engaging with the guest.

2. There are three fields of operation where you have the opportunity to be fully present: mental, physical, and emotional. Excellent hospitality requires relating to the guest in each of those areas.

3. Here are six practical ways to be fully present:

   a. Watch your body language.

   b. Intermittently repeat back what you are hearing your guest say.

   c. Be emotionally intelligent.

   d. Understand your role in the big picture.

   e. Personalize the experience.

   f. Accomplish your tasks early.

five

Think Scene by Scene

Businesses like to think in terms of functions. For instance, consider a hotel. Who will check people in? Who will clean the rooms? Who will fix food and drinks? These are all roles that need staffing.

So the hotel looks for a check-in team, a housekeeping team, and a kitchen staff. They are assigned the tasks of welcoming people and making them feel comfortable.

Unfortunately, the guest doesn't think like this. They have no idea of all the tasks someone at the check-in desk performs. They don't know what it's like for housekeeping staff or kitchen staff outside of their basic roles. Instead, the guest thinks in terms of scenes. Their thought process looks something like this:

Scene 1: The Drive or Ride to the Hotel
Scene 2: Finding a Parking Spot or Visiting the Valet
Scene 3: Walking to the Front Doors

Scene 4: Navigating the Lobby

Scene 5: Visiting the Public Restroom

Scene 6: Checking In

Scene 7: Navigating the Hallways

Scene 8: Finding and Riding in the Elevator

Scene 9: Entering the Room

Scene 10: Exiting the Room and Navigating the Hallways Again

Scene 11: Riding in the Elevator Again

Scene 12: Navigating the Lobby Again

Scene 13: Finding Their Car

Scene 14: Driving to Their Destination

You see, for them, visiting a hotel is an adventure story akin to *The Lord of the Rings*—especially if it's their first time.

They're on a journey, much like Frodo with his ring. Along the way, there will be inconveniences and stress points. Those along the path will either become allies, obstacles, or enemies. And each new scene they encounter will either be a place of healing or a place of hostility.

What will your business be in this story? Will it be Mordor—a place of dangers and stress? Will it be Rivendell—a place of healing?

What will your role be in the story? Will you be an Orc—someone adding stress and anxiety to the situation? Will you be a Sam—someone easing their burden?

Just like *The Lord of the Rings*, each scene of your business is a moment of potential conflict. The guest is wondering,

Will I have to wait in a long line for the valet, or will I be able to find a parking spot? Will the lobby be easy to find? Will they have my reservation, or will there be problems? Is this hotel safe and in a safe part of town? Will the room be clean? Will I be able to find the room?

They don't care if a certain cone has been put out in the parking lot. They don't care if all three receptionists are at the check-in counter. They certainly don't care if that bowl of mints was placed out by the complimentary coffee in the lobby. They're just thinking about which rooms and spaces they'll have to visit. If you look at the scene list above, that's quite a few spaces. And there are plenty of other rooms that we didn't include.

Each of those spaces complicates the process and creates a potential for conflict. Your job in extending hospitality is to ease those points of tension. The crazy thing about it is that some of these scenes are outside of your control. But for the guest, they are still all part of visiting your business.

JASON

At one of the organizations I worked with, we navigated this idea for events. We had been trying to decide where our control of the guest experience begins. We understood that several roads feed our location, but there is one major entry point that requires more attention than any other.

When a guest pulls off Highway 400, they turn onto Lenox Road and turn left onto Tower Place Drive. The building is right there, with its 320 dedicated parking spaces and three rented parking decks that surround it. Because vehicles are entering and leaving the parking decks, our control obviously starts on Tower Place Drive. We're creating the traffic chaos, so we need to manage it for the guest. But even more than that, our control begins on Lenox Road—at the long red light that awaits the guest. Obviously, we can't do much about the length of the light other than staff it with highway patrol who can direct traffic, but we're constantly looking for ways we can help the guest navigate that scene of their journey.

The next scene? Looking for a parking spot. Again, we can't control the other drivers in our decks, but we do our best to ease the tension of this scene through our parking team.

During every incremental scene, it was important to ask, "What is the guest thinking and feeling?" Then we did our best to anticipate their needs in each scene.

One simple way we anticipated needs is by understanding that if the guest is a parent with an infant or a preschool-age child, they carry other items with them. Therefore, we wanted to make the walk as easy as possible for them and provide a shorter distance for them to walk. They saw street signs that told them to put their flashers on, and we guided them to park in the deck underneath the building. There we had an express elevator for them to get into the building.

JONATHAN

One of the businesses I run is a social media graphics company. We have a Netflix model where you can subscribe and download as many graphics as you want to use on your social media accounts.

Even though we have a great search system, I try to make it especially easy for people to find what they need. I anticipate what they might need every day and update the home page to reflect that.

For each day of the year, I've created a calendar with "National Day of . . ." or holidays and famous people's birthdays. Then I deliver suggested posts for each of those special events.

We do this in an attempt to guess what our website's guests want before they even get there. Ideally, a guest would never have to search or scroll through our organization system. When we anticipate what the guest wants beforehand, it shows that we understand them and are allies in what they're trying to accomplish.

Breaking Down the Scenes

What are the different scenes in your business? Where does one scene stop and another start? For each organization, the breakdown of the scenes will be different.

The natural place to start is with location. Go to Google Maps and grab an aerial shot of your building or draw a diagram of your area. Walk through the process of a guest who is choosing to visit your location. (Use your demographic/ psychographic information—their family, their age, and so forth—to inform you of what your guest will need to do while they're there.) What happens when they first pull into the parking lot? Then what happens when they walk to the front door?

The first part of this scene-by-scene process is, naturally, your building. Your rooms, doors, and hallways will determine what different scenes your guest encounters. If your building is blessed with good architecture, this might not be a challenge for your guest. But if the layout of the building and the rooms is confusing, this becomes an obstacle. What will you do to help people overcome these obstacles and get to the next scene?

The second part is what you create. For instance, by putting team members in certain locations, you might actually be placing a barrier in the guest's mind. Some people don't want to have to talk to someone or shake someone's hand on their way to the restrooms. Some people don't want to deal with a gauntlet of salespeople as soon as they enter the building. The structures we create might be the very thing adding difficulty to the story.

The third part of the scene-by-scene process is what the guest assumes. Depending on their background, they'll naturally imagine certain scenes based on their past experiences. Those might be either things they're looking forward to or things they're dreading (like a team member approaching them, or waiting in line). They might be sensitive to certain verbiage. Or they might be waiting to be pressured into purchasing something they aren't sure they need.

Breaking down the scenes in your guest experience helps you see where there are gaps in their visit. It helps you identify moments of decision or conflict. (And there *are* moments of decision and conflict in each scene, whether you identify them or not.)

What if, instead of a moment of conflict, you could re-create something about the way the guest thinks, feels, and assumes? For instance, a moment of conflict might be getting their bags up to their hotel room, though the conflict is often far more complicated than that. What if the guest is distrustful of someone handling their bags? What if they forgot to bring cash to tip the person carrying their bags? What if they're weak from an injury and carrying their bags is a challenge for them? You don't know what's behind each request or each situation that might make a commonplace thing an obstacle.

What if you could make a scene memorable? Can you think of an opportunity to create a moment that surprises and delights your guest? Let's explore this idea of "surprise and delight" a little further.

Surprise and Delight

There's a fine balance between predictability and surprise. People like predictability because it's safe—especially for a generation who experienced COVID-19. Making sure things are clean and giving people a good amount of personal space are important for a generation that lived through a pandemic.

So when we talk about creating moments of surprise and delight in the scenes at businesses, we're talking about moments that don't bring a disruption to the guest's comfort level. For instance, it could be something simple like fruit-infused water instead of regular water in the lobby. Or it could be something like providing Cracker Jacks and glass Coke bottles if there's a big baseball game happening in your community. It's about doing something people didn't see coming that fits within a framework of comfort.

Businesses already do this all the time: free dessert if it's your birthday, bonus room upgrades at a hotel, or packing a little toy or sticker in a shipped package. It's in those extras that you have the opportunity to surprise and delight.

Sometimes your greatest opportunity to provide a little extra—something the customer wasn't expecting—is when something goes wrong. Because we all have stories in the forefront of our minds of bad experiences with companies, we tend to remember and even be surprised when a company makes things right. Surprisingly, it's when your business has to say no to a customer (a word no customer likes to hear) that you can create a real sense of surprise and delight.

JASON

Recently we were picking up a prescription for one of my children at our local pharmacy. When the pharmacist told us the price, it was way higher than we were expecting. Not only that, but it had to be refilled two more times.

The pharmacist noticed my surprise, and she showed immediate empathy. She didn't show annoyance. She didn't make me feel cheap for not wanting to pay the amount. Instead, she offered to look something up for me.

When she came back, she told me about a different pharmacy down the street. She showed me that the price was two-thirds less there than at her pharmacy. She even Air-Dropped a coupon to my phone that would bring the price down further.

Now, while that might seem like she was being disloyal to her pharmacy, it actually communicated something different: loyalty toward me, the customer. So besides this one prescription, can you guess what my preferred pharmacy will be from now on? Yep—the one where the employee showed me loyalty and care. By sending me to another store, she actually earned my loyalty more than she would have if I had purchased the prescription from her location.

She couldn't help me with the price at her store, but she could help me another way.

It's in those "no" situations that you will most often find the opportunity to create a moment of surprise and delight for a guest. When you can work around a restrictive policy and make the guest feel uniquely valued, you have created a "wow" in the guest's mind. That's memorable.

Transitioning Scenes

One part of great storytelling is creating great scenes. But the story becomes choppy if the storyteller doesn't easily transition between the scenes. Your goal in hospitality is to help your guests transition seamlessly between the various scenes they'll encounter.

It's obvious when an organization doesn't think through this scene-transition element. You've probably dealt with this on a support call to a company. When you call to make a purchase, you get the A-level phone bank workers. They're quick and responsive to every request you have. But then, when you call back in a week or so to report a problem, the phone bank worker says, "You'll need to talk to our support staff." Then they give you a phone number to call their outsourced support branch. You call and have to restate your problem. The customer support employees do their best to be helpful, but ultimately there isn't much they can do. The transition between your first scene (purchasing the product) and your next scene (product support) was choppy.

As the customer, you don't think in terms of roles. You don't think about the difference between sales and support staff. You just want help. But since the company hasn't done a good job of working out the transitions between scenes, they've created a bad experience for you. They've forced you to have to adapt to the organization's system instead of the system adapting to you, the customer.

Imagine if you called a company's support line and got help from the first person who took your call. Sure, they might have to say, "Let me get in touch with our support staff and get that fixed for you. Can I put you on a brief hold?" But you'd gladly hold, knowing someone's taking care of the problem without you having to jump through organizational hoops.

Now imagine this idea of transitioning scenes applied to your business. Using a hotel as an example, what would it look like to create a seamless end-to-end experience?

1. A guest pulls into the parking lot, and a parking attendant guides them to the closest available spot: the one that's most obvious to the guest . . . not the spot that's most convenient for the parking attendant's system.

2. The guest exits their car and sees a sign over the entrance making it clear where they need to go next. They don't have to guess where the main entrance is.

3. The guest enters the lobby, and the receptionist welcomes them and beckons them over, knowing that they're there to check in. (The parking lot attendant signaled to the team member.)

4. The team member gets the guest checked in and offers someone to help them take their bags up to the room, with no pressure either way. Since the guest is

holding a baby, the team member anticipates that a refrigerator will be needed, so they mention there's one in every room already.

5. The team member suggests a great place to eat since it's getting close to dinnertime.
6. The team member invites the guest to call them if they have any other questions.

In the above scenario, there isn't a point where the guest even needs to ask a question. The team members and the signage anticipated what the guest would need in each scene and helped them transition seamlessly between scenes.

While it might not be feasible for your team to function like that completely, the principle still applies. The goal is to keep the guest from even having to ask the obvious questions. Sure, there will always be random questions that are impossible to anticipate. But when you are quick enough to answer the questions you *can* anticipate, the guest will feel comfortable asking the ones you *can't*.

It's important to note that the goal is not to shuffle people through the scenes as fast as possible. Hospitality is a process, but you shouldn't make your guest *feel* processed.

JONATHAN

Have you ever been through the ordering line at Chipotle? They're masters at processing through customers. They ask you questions before you've even had the chance to make a request. (White rice or brown? Black beans or pinto? What kind of meat do you want?) It's even a fun game I've played once or twice—trying to state my order before they've had the chance to ask. I've never succeeded in beating them to the punch. They're good. And while that works great for a quick-service restaurant, it doesn't work so well for a business.

⸻

You want to make transitioning scenes a simple process, but you don't want to rush people through the procedure. Put the power in the guest's hands. Let them progress through as slowly or as quickly as they like. Remember, if you're new to a place, it takes a while to take everything in. Let the guest absorb the sights and sounds without rushing them through the activity.

Whose Story Is It Anyway?

Each time we open the doors of our business, we're telling a story to our guest. Either it will be an exciting story with a happy ending, or it'll be a tragedy that leaves our guests unwilling to return the next time. Obviously we want to tell a good story. And while it might be tempting to tell a story about our business, the story of our hospitality is about someone else.

One of the greatest perspective shifts we can make in hospitality is understanding who the hero of the story actually is. As staff members, we find it natural to put ourselves in that hero role. We want to be the protagonist of the story. But if we're going to be truly excellent at hospitality, we have to take a supporting role. The true hero of the story is the guest. Their visit to the business is *their* story.

The question we have to ask ourselves is this: Will we be a villain in the guest's story, an inconvenient obstacle, or an ally?

There will be plenty of villains in their story, like the guy who runs the red light on their drive to your location. There will be inconvenient obstacles, like their kids who are tired and getting grumpy. Your guest doesn't need any more villains or obstacles. A come back culture is choosing to be the ally in their story.

Don't just greet your guest. Be their ally. Or if you aren't the person to do that, connect them with the right people. Introduce them to a friend who will help them get where they need to go.

They need an ally. They need someone who will help them overcome these obstacles. They need someone they can rely on who will help them reach the happy ending of their story.

It's too easy to think about our own story. We get lost in our own obstacles and our own villains. *Did the night shift close things up properly and prepare for today? Is my breath bad? Did Tom ever show up for his position, or am I going to have to do his job too?* While these obstacles do matter, we can't afford to think about our story when it's time to welcome guests. We have to be fully focused on helping them tell *their* story.

Is your hospitality set up in such a way that the hero of your story can get from scene to scene without a massive battle or crisis? Is your team positioned in such a way that a guest will feel comfortable asking for help—no matter how intimidating that request might be?

JASON

I do a lot of my grocery shopping at Publix. Recently when I was shopping, an employee was restocking cereal boxes. Normally when you approach an employee at a grocery store, they tend to ignore you and keep at their task. It can be intimidating to ask them a question.

This employee, however, saw me approaching and acknowledged me. "I'm sorry I'm in your way. Is there anything I can help you find?"

She actually stopped her immediate task and devoted her attention to me. It would have been easy for her to assume her job was stocking shelves. But in that moment, she acknowledged that the bigger purpose of her job was to assist the grocery store's guests. Even by stocking the shelves, she was helping me find what I needed. So when she could do that in a more personal way, she took the opportunity.

This is something I've noticed about Publix. Their slogan is "Where shopping is a pleasure." It reminds me of something Horst Schulze, former CEO of Ritz-Carlton, told me one time: "If you know what you promise, then you can deliver it consistently."

When you get lost in your role, you miss out on opportunities like this. A guest doesn't care about your role. They don't care if your job is to refill mints or restock shelves. They really just want to know that you're there for them. Guests pay attention to who you are, not what you do.

Ask yourself these questions: *Am I the type of person who will stop what I'm doing to be fully present for a guest? Is the guest the hero in my eyes?*

At each scene in your business, does the guest feel like they belong? Do they feel like you've done the difficult work of creating scenes that make it easy for them to get where they need to go? Will they want to come back—to relive this story each time they visit your business?

Key Points and Takeaways

1. Guests don't think in terms of tasks or roles; they think in terms of scenes and barriers to where they want to go. One of your most important jobs in hospitality is to remove those barriers.

2. The primary barriers your guests will experience are based on the physical location and arrangement of your building, your own organizational structure and red tape, and your guests' assumptions about what they will experience.

3. Make the experience of a guest's visit safe and predictable. However, when it doesn't negatively affect the guest's comfort level, add moments of surprise and delight.

4. A guest's experience should feel seamless—not departmental and choppy. Make the handoff between your business's roles feel like one big experience instead of many small ones.

5. Your guest is the hero in the story of their visit; your role is the ally.

six

Recover Quickly

JASON

As you can tell, I like Disney World. A few years ago, I took some leaders to Disney World for an immersive experience. Now, I don't ride roller coasters, but everyone who came with me did. So I held their bags and purses while they rode the Rock 'N' Roller Coaster. The wait time on the ride said twenty minutes, so we expected it to be a short experience. However, forty minutes came and went and there was still no sign of the others. At first I thought they were playing a trick on me and just hiding at the exit. When I finally realized that wasn't the case, I started to worry.

We had fast passes to see *Beauty and the Beast*, an experience a few people in our group *really* wanted to see. It was our last day there and this showing was the last one, so it was our only chance.

I looked for a cast member, and when I encountered Maria, I told her about the situation. She owned the moment. She took me behind the scenes, outside of where guests were normally allowed to be, and helped me find my group in line for the roller coaster. She called over to the Beauty and the Beast attraction to make sure we would still be able to make it. Then she walked us over there and made sure we were seated before the musical started.

Before she left us, though, Maria gave us fast passes to come back to the roller coaster after the musical. Not only did she recover in the moment, apologizing that the wait-time clock was broken, but she also got us to the place we needed to go and gave us an opportunity to get back to the roller coaster as well. That was an amazing recovery.

Even in the midst of serving customers well, things can go wrong. People get their feelings hurt or we fail to meet their expectations. And it's up to us to make things right. A come back culture is about recovering, and recovering quickly.

Why do we focus on recovering quickly? Is it to make the guest feel better? Yes, but that's a by-product. When we recover well with the guest, we show them loyalty. By being loyal to them, we open the door for them to be loyal back toward us. After all, customer loyalty isn't a one-sided experience. It's not just something we get from the customer. It's a mutual trust that develops over time.

Think of one of the brands you're most loyal toward. There's a good chance something went wrong in your dealings with the company and they had to make something right for you. We're willing to bet that the strongest cord of your loyalty with that company was developed in the way they recovered from something that went wrong.

Things will happen. What will we do to make them right?

Preparing for Recovery

There are three major truths when it comes to hospitality in business:

1. You aren't perfect (even though you're striving for it).
2. The guest is not perfect.
3. Something will go wrong.

While those three truths might read negatively, acknowledging them isn't being pessimistic. In customer service, you hope for the best, but you also prepare for the worst. No matter how flawless your hospitality systems and team members are, things go wrong. Understanding this helps you put plans into place and prepare to recover.

JASON

In 2020, I engaged with a golf company called Peter Millar. I bought two golf vests (I realize Jonathan will probably make fun of me for this). There was also a promo for a free Bluetooth speaker with a purchase, valued at $30.

Well, a global pandemic hit. I realized I probably shouldn't be buying expensive golf vests, especially when I wasn't sure when I'd be able to play golf next.

I emailed Peter Millar to return the vests, and they were gracious. They informed me that returning the vests would be no problem and that they understood. They didn't make me feel guilty. In fact, the representative took it a step further. She told me to return the vests but to keep the Bluetooth speaker.

"No, no," I said. "It's my fault. You guys didn't do anything wrong. I made the mistake buying something and realizing I shouldn't keep it."

"Keep it," she said. "Enjoy it. We'll be here when things change."

I thought that was an incredible recovery, even though the company actually had nothing to recover from. They realized that the guest (and the global pandemic) created the problem, but they still took it on themselves to fix it.

Not every company has profit margins that allow them to do something like that. We acknowledge that. But the point is that when a customer is feeling the pain of a mistake, businesses have the opportunity to recover. The best brands don't worry that a customer might be at fault or even taking advantage of the company; they just recover.

Preparing to recover is about acknowledging things will happen and doing your best to quickly make things right. What can you do to prepare for the worst? The first step is knowing the three areas where something can go wrong:

1. With a team member
2. With a guest
3. With the process

A team member or staff member might accidentally offend the guest. The guest might simply be having a bad day. Or there might be a restrictive rule that causes the guest inconvenience.

Every problem from which you'll need to recover comes from one or a combination of those three things. If you don't know them, you can't set up something proactive to deal with a problem that arises.

Put a plan into action with your team. Give them some of the tools you'll find later in this chapter to help them deal with the emotions of the situation. Consider the following:

- Some hotels give their employees an allowance to use at their discretion to help the customer.
- Some restaurants give servers the option to comp a meal or offer a free dessert.
- Some subscription companies offer free months of membership or cool bonuses to make up for issues.

Sometimes the best preparation you can have is to simply know something might happen so you can prepare yourself emotionally for it. You know things will go wrong, so prepare yourself and your team for the potential.

It's important to note that even though there are three areas where something can go wrong, we can do something about only two of them. We can fix the team member or we can fix the process. But we can't necessarily fix the guest. One of the big mistakes people make in customer service, though, is to try to fix the customer.

JONATHAN

One of the worst guest experiences I've ever had was at a gymnastics school. The owner failed at recovery—miserably. My wife and I had purchased a summer program for her thirteen-year-old sister. She was staying with us for the summer, and we didn't want her bored at home while we were at work.

We found out after the first day, though, that the summer program was geared more toward children under the age of nine. The program mostly involved coloring and watching the Disney Channel, with only a few minutes of basic gymnastics activities during the day.

So instead of dropping off my sister-in-law the next day, I stayed with her until the owner showed up. I wanted to see if there was some way I could at least get a partial refund since she did attend the camp for one day.

When the owner finally arrived, I approached the situation as calmly as possible. Having read *How to Win Friends and Influence People*, I put on my best Dale Carnegie charm and told her I thought the program might be a bit age inappropriate for my sister-in-law. "I don't expect to get a full refund for what we paid," I said, "but I was wondering if I could at least get a refund for the rest of the days."

The owner had apparently never read *How to Win Friends and Influence People*, because she didn't get what I was trying to do. And she certainly didn't respond in a way that made me want to be her friend. Her body language was one of annoyance, and she responded in kind. "I don't know if you can get a refund. I'll have to look at it."

She doesn't know? "Okay . . . So should I leave my sister-in-law here? We did pay for it, so I don't want to waste the money if we can't get a refund."

"I can't tell you that, sir."

"Okay . . . Well, can you at least let me know when you'll know whether or not I can get a refund? I'm just trying to plan my day and figure out what to do here. I don't mean to cause you undue trouble."

"Sir, I told you I can't tell you," she said. "I've already told you, and as the owner of this establishment, I have the right to remove you from these premises."

Whoa, that escalated quickly. The situation devolved from there. I'm ashamed to say I lost a bit of my rationality and left the encounter physically trembling with anger.

The owner of this company was trying to recover by changing me. I had a problem first with the process, but she wasn't willing to change that. Then I had a problem with a team member (her), but she wasn't willing to change that either. She was trying to fix me, and that wasn't an option.

———

You can't fix a customer. You can't fix your guest. They are the focal point, not the problem. You can only do your best to fix other things in order to recover.

That story was obviously an example of how not to make something right. So how do you go about recovering the right way?

How to Make It Right

There are two types of situations you'll encounter when it comes to recovering with a guest. The first is a reasonable guest who has a justifiable complaint because something went wrong. The faster you resolve these situations, the less emotions will fly around. The second situation is someone whose anger has turned irrational; they have let their emotions go beyond the point of logic. At that point, there's no easy solution. They're looking to rage against the situation.

You aren't likely to fix the situation if it's devolved into irrationality. In the next section, we'll talk about some strategies for dealing with irrational guests. But for now, we'll talk about the first situation, because that one can actually be made right.

The first step to making something right when a guest has a complaint is to deal with the feelings first, then deal with the problem. We talked about this in an earlier chapter. Once a situation arises in which there needs to be recovery, the guest has already begun experiencing the feelings you don't want them to. It becomes an emotional issue instead of just a logical one. And you can't hope to deal with the logic until the emotions have been pacified.

After you acknowledge and address the emotions, then you can start to deal with the situation. That might mean someone else needs to deal with it, because the guest associates the emotion with the person. Regardless of who approaches the situation to resolve it, there are seven steps to making things right. These steps apply to most situations and can ensure a level of excellence in your care for guests.

1. Listen

When someone has a complaint, they've often spent a significant amount of time rehearsing in their head what they plan to say. Let them say it. Let them get it all out. Otherwise you're short-circuiting what they've been rehearsing, and you leave the emotion inside them.

Pardon the gross analogy, but their complaint is like a substance inside of them that needs to get out. They need to vomit it, in a sense. And if you don't let them get it all out, it just sits inside of them and continues to make them sick. Fully hear them out before you continue. Let your listening ear be a healing touch to the emotions inside of them. Once the emotion is out, then you can start working on the solution.

2. Review

One of the best ways to show someone that you're listening is to repeat back to them what they've said. Voice their concerns in your own words so you can guarantee you are both on the same page. Don't patronize them; seek to truly understand.

3. Empathize

Hear first, then feel. You don't have a right to craft a response until the guest is done airing their grievance. Then empathize before you respond. If you're honest, you'd probably feel the same way they do if you were in their shoes. Feel the emotion they feel.

Often the situation is fully resolved here. Sometimes empathy is all the guest wants. For some people, the emotions are the full extent of the problems. And knowing they are affirmed in what they feel goes a long way.

4. Apologize

Take responsibility even if you don't feel responsible. Even if someone else caused the problem or you feel the guest is unjustified in their emotions, apologize. And don't try to get clever with your response by saying something like,

"I'm sorry you got offended by this." That shifts the blame back onto the guest for feeling the way they do instead of you taking responsibility. People can sense when you aren't being genuine.

5. Resolve

Often, restitution isn't perfect. If there was a time limit on the experience or if an opportunity passed by, there's nothing you can do to recover that lost time. But you can still do your best to resolve the emotions of the situation.

One of the most empowering things you can do for a guest who feels wronged is to offer them options for restitution. "We want to make this right. We could do _____ or _____. Which would you prefer?" This makes the resolution feel more customized for the guest. (Of course, this means a team member needs to be armed with any options that are on the table.)

Make sure, too, that you resolve the actual situation as much as possible. The goal isn't just to throw irrelevant options at the customer. The measure of the resolution should match the measure of the offense.

6. Follow Up

It's important to care in the moment. But if you want to take it to the next level, care after the fact. Follow up with the guest by giving them a call or finding them after their problem was fixed. People don't necessarily expect follow-up after their problems are resolved, but it's great when it happens.

Make sure this doesn't come from a self-serving motivation. For instance, some car dealerships are great at following up with a phone call after they've performed service on your car: "We just wanted to make sure you were happy with the service you received. . . . You are? Good! Well, you might receive a call in a couple of days with a survey asking how we did. We'd love it if you rated us five stars across the board."

Those last two sentences ruined the follow-up. It took what was a nice, caring act and turned it into a self-serving one.

7. Discuss

Turn the recovery into a learning opportunity. Write down what happened, then review it with your team in a meeting or an email. This will help you refine your process and prepare for future times when this sort of recovery might be necessary. If you can learn something from one person who had a bad experience, next week you can proactively prepare so somebody else doesn't have the same experience.

Follow those seven steps and you'll have the best chance at turning a bad situation into a positive experience. If you're doing it right, you should never hear these words coming out of your mouth:

- "Calm down."
    This sort of statement is demeaning.
- "That's not my problem."
    It's important to take ownership.
- "You're being irrational."
    If they weren't already irrational, this statement will make them be.

- "What's your problem?"
  If you ask this, you just made yourself their problem.
- "That's against our policy."
  This shows the guest that policy takes precedence over them.
- "I'll try to do that."
  This answer feels noncommittal, like you'll try if you remember to try.
- "Let me know if you have any other problems."
  This implies the guest will likely have more problems. If you handled their problem well, they will come back to you. Instead, maybe say, "Let me know if there's any other way I can help!"
- "I don't know."
  Neither do they. It's your job to figure it out.

If you say any of the things above, you'll probably turn your guest into an irrational one. Instead, you should hear yourself say:

- "I can see how you feel [insert emotion]."
- "I can imagine that is [insert emotion]."
- "How may I help you today?"
- "I can help."
- "Thank you for letting me help take care of you today."
- "I don't know the answer, but I want to and will find out for you."

- "I am sorry." (With no "but" added.)
- "What I can do for you right now is _____."

Recovering well from a bad situation can be one of the most challenging parts of hospitality in business. But if it's done right, it can turn a bad situation into an excellent one. It's when things go wrong that there's the greatest opportunity to forge a meaningful and memorable connection.

Often the best relationships are forged through adversity. When you are willing to humble yourself and make things right, that's when people open their hearts to you. Even though you might have dropped the ball, making things right will turn your guest into a superfan.

- "I love this coffee shop because when someone stole my drink from the counter, they didn't just remake it for me. They gave me a coupon for a free drink in the future."
- "I love this store because they refunded my money before they even received the product back in the mail."
- "I love this airline because they went above and beyond. They lost my bag and could have just had me return to the airport to pick it up. But instead they sent an employee an hour across town to deliver it."

Irrational Guests

Finally, how do you deal with a guest who crosses the point of no return? When there seems to be no hope for the situation, how do you respond?

First, it's important to acknowledge your own feelings. You have them. They are real. If someone's yelling at you, you're probably going to feel like the brown stuff on the bottom of a shoe. But at the same time, you can't let your own feelings interfere with what's going on right now.

You aren't just a tool of the organization. Obviously someone expressing their anger will affect your mood. But you also have a responsibility to rise above what you're feeling and provide hospitality to the guest.

Holly Stiel, in *The Art and Science of the Hotel Concierge*,[1] offers nine tips for helping an angry guest:

1. **"Remain calm and patient."** There's an ancient proverb that tells us, "A gentle answer deflects anger, but harsh words make tempers flare."[2] If you allow your words to become too intense, you're simply adding gasoline to the fire of what they're feeling. Be gentle in your response.

2. **"Feel confident."** Sometimes people fear an irrational guest. Maybe you don't think there's any hope for this type of person. But you were trusted with your role. Don't fear contact with this type of person. You can do it.

3. **"Don't become defensive or intimidated."** Don't let someone intimidate you in your role. You have authority in this situation, even though a yelling guest might make you feel otherwise. You don't have to defend yourself. You don't have to yell. And you certainly don't have to shrink back. True authority removes the need to be defensive.

4. **"Never be condescending to a guest."** Remember, your guest has value beyond what they do for your company. They aren't just a buyer of your product. When you condescend to a guest, you strip away that value. Let your body language, tone, and even what you *don't* say reinforce their value in the eyes of your company.

5. **"Avoid offering excuses."** People don't necessarily care why something happened—especially when they've gotten to this point. Logic never fixes feelings, so don't offer excuses. Own the situation.

6. **"Don't blame other departments or individuals for the problem."** People don't care who was at fault. But more than that, if you blame other departments or individuals, you show disloyalty. It's a form of contempt for the business when you point fingers.

7. **"It's never appropriate to argue with a guest."** Arguments don't add anything positive to the experience. The only reason people feel the need to argue is because of a desire for self-preservation or because they want to be right. It's an ego thing. And if this is about your ego, you're not doing hospitality; you're serving yourself. You might consider moving with the guest to a more comfortable and personal location, away from the stress of people looking on, and connect in a casual way instead of a formal one.

8. **"Avoid asking too many questions until the guest has had an opportunity to vent."** People need to get out the emotion before they can process the logic of the situation. Don't chime in too fast. Just listen. Let the

117

guest take control of the conversation until they're ready to turn over control to you. This might mean sitting and listening even when everything inside you wants to hurry along the conversation. But the best thing you can do in this situation is let the guest vent.

9. **"Remember: It's not about you."** Don't take it personally. The guest is not really attacking you, as much as it might feel like it. Even when the guest uses words that feel completely *ad hominem*—words like "you guys" or "you"—the situation is not about you. It's about what the guest feels. Remove yourself from the equation and deal with the situation.

Recovery is one of the hardest parts of a come back culture. It's emotionally draining and uncomfortable. But the biggest "wows" you will ever get—the most memorable moments guests will have with your business—will come from properly dealing with these sorts of problems that arise.

Every great story we tell has conflict. Something goes wrong. We don't love a story where nothing happens. Instead, we love to see the journey of a hero making things right. So don't be afraid of conflict; prepare to create a come back culture by making things right.

Key Points and Takeaways

1. There will be times when you unintentionally ruin an experience for a guest. Acknowledge that it will happen and prepare for it.

2. You aren't perfect and the guest isn't perfect either, but you can only control the first part. You can't control the guest.

3. Knowing a breakdown in hospitality will occur, give your team tools to help make things right when something does go wrong.

4. When something goes wrong for a guest, listen to their feelings first, then deal with the situation.

5. Follow these seven steps (in order) to make things right: listen, review with the guest what you think they said, empathize, apologize, resolve, follow up with the guest, and discuss the situation with the team so you can learn from it.

6. If the guest becomes irrational because of the situation, there's a good chance there will be no clean resolution. All you can do is humble yourself, listen, and avoid becoming defensive.

seven

Observe Details, Because Everything Communicates

I'm sure you remember the fictional character Sherlock Holmes. He was an English detective created by Sir Arthur Conan Doyle. He had a knack for walking into a crime scene and seeing things nobody else saw. Even the most seemingly insignificant details told him a clear narrative of what happened at a crime scene.

Although none of us are probably quite as astute as Mr. Holmes, we all adopt his methodologies at times—even if only on a subconscious level. For instance, think of the last time you walked into a room where it was obvious an argument had just occurred. Both of the arguers probably stopped talking as soon as they heard you open the door. But some subtle clues in the room indicated what had just happened. You could see micro facial expressions. You could see flushed faces. There was a certain cold courtesy in the way the two interacted with each other. They were trying to pretend like nothing had happened, but every single one of those details communicated to you a different story. Even if only subconsciously, most everyone can pick up on those small signals and piece together a story explaining what might have happened.

Just like everything communicates in a crime scene or in a room in which an argument just occurred, everything communicates to your guest. Every small detail they encounter when they engage with your business tells them a story—even if it's a story contrary to what you're hoping to tell.

What does the flow of customer service communicate to the guest? What does your team communicate? What does your building or room design communicate?

JONATHAN

One thing that always bugs me about restaurants is the restroom. I've been in great restrooms, but those seem to be rare. Even at great restaurants, the restrooms are usually an afterthought to the experience.

A simple representation of this is the soap dispenser. Nearly every restaurant starts with official soap dispensers that they bought from a restaurant supply company. But somewhere along the line, so many decide not to pay for the refills for the dispensers mounted to the walls. Instead, they opt for a bottle of soap they purchase at their local grocery store. Then, somewhere along the line, they decide they don't want to purchase new bottles of soap when refills are needed, so they purchase the cheapest kind of refill you can get at a Sam's Club or Walmart. I can tell the smell from a mile away.

Now, that might seem nitpicky. But when I push the dispenser on the wall and nothing comes out, then move to the bottle of soap that isn't even dispensing the brand the bottle advertises, it says a lot to me about the restaurant. It tells me they look for opportunities to cut corners wherever they can. If they do that with something as inexpensive as hand soap, how much more are they doing that with the ingredients they use in my meal?

In *The Starbucks Experience*, Joseph Michelli says, "If you ignore the smaller things that are important to those you serve, you'll fail to create the experience they crave."[1] People crave care and they crave excellence. Is the flow of your business communicating those values?

JASON

The same Ritz-Carlton that accommodated my checkout needs thoroughly impressed me with their attention to other small details. Down in the pool area, there was a restroom between the pool and the exercise area. Normally, you wouldn't expect much from a restroom there. In fact, you might assume it would be pretty disgusting, between all the sweat and chlorinated water that probably dripped all over the facilities. But I noticed this restroom was in impeccable condition.

Even the quality of the paper towels I used to dry my hands impressed me. They were a thicker, expensive quality. In this area where they could have gotten away with something cheaper, they didn't. And that communicated so much to me. Something as simple as paper towels in a bathroom communicated excellence.

Often, businesses are known for cutting costs. After all, the goal of a business is to maximize profit, so you need to minimize expenses. But when you choose the easy way out, it communicates a lower level of care to your guests. It communicates that "just okay" is acceptable. Who wants to go to a *just okay* restaurant? A *just okay* hotel? A *just okay* mechanic shop? A *just okay* hair salon? In the long term, cutting costs can hurt more than help if it's communicating the wrong thing to the guest.

Every part of your business communicates to the guest. *Everything.* Here are a few things that might be talking to your guest:

- **The volume of the ambient music in the room.** If it's too loud, it communicates the place is a raucous party. If it's too soft, it communicates the place is a funeral.
- **The colors you paint the walls.** Colors evoke certain emotions in people's minds. What emotions do your walls evoke? Serenity? Anger? Passivity? Excitement?
- **Where you put the trash bags.** Are they sitting next to the garbage cans? It's convenient to those taking out the garbage, but it communicates laziness to the guest.
- **Ingredients for food items visible to the customer.** While it's not reasonable to assume your baristas or kitchen staff will know the recipe to every item on the menu when they're new to the staff, not posting signage with the ingredients in locations visible to the customer communicates that nobody knows what

they're doing. It can make a guest worry that their food or drink won't be made correctly. It sets expectations low before they even get what they ordered.

- **The smells in the room.** Those special mini quiches you serve to your guests may taste great . . . or the popcorn your team member made on their break may be perfectly reasonable . . . but if the kitchen is close to where people will gather, it might stink up the whole room. Unless you're a restaurant or a concession stand, smells like those can seem incongruous with what your business is trying to accomplish.

The Importance of Intentionality

Understanding that everything communicates means you need to plan ahead. It's easy to simply make decisions in the moment because decisions *have to* be made. But when you don't make decisions with intentionality, you can't easily control what those decisions will communicate.

The problem is, most people don't notice intentionality. It's easy to think some things just happen. Take, for instance, the FedEx logo. By now, you've probably discovered the hidden arrow between the last *e* and the *x* of the logo. (If not, google the FedEx logo. We'll wait.) The white space between the two letters creates an arrow pointing to the right. Do you think that was simply a happy accident? Most people probably imagine the designers opening Photoshop, writing out the word "FedEx," and noticing the arrow it created. "Sweet! Let's make this word two different colors, then ship it off to the marketing director!" Most of us think the designers created the whole logo in less than an hour.

It's easy to imagine that happening because that's often how things happen in business. Faced with constant, staggering deadlines, we often rely on happy accidents rather than painstaking intentionality.

The truth is, though, the company that worked on the FedEx logo consisted of two or three teams that developed around two hundred concepts for the logo. Some included arrows in the designs, but a simple arrow in a logo didn't communicate what they wanted. The designer, instead, combined two fonts to get the hidden arrow that communicated the story he wanted to tell through the logo. Then he tweaked and re-spaced and re-formed the letters until he got the shape he desired. When he sent it to the bigwigs at FedEx, corporate wanted to make the arrow a bigger deal. They wanted to use the arrow on print pieces and focus on it. But the designer never wanted it to be about the arrow. The arrow was merely a detail that communicated—one of many. And through this high attention to detail, it's still one of the most celebrated logos in history.[2]

What's most interesting about the FedEx logo is that the arrow technically isn't there. It's visible only in the white space. Sometimes, what you *don't* do communicates just as much as what you *do*. What isn't in the picture is just as important as what is. Intentionality takes into account every single element of the experience.

It's easy for people to plan ahead when it comes to big-picture things only. They know generally what will happen during a visit to a business. And that's good. We've all been to businesses that obviously haven't even planned the big-picture stuff. But very few businesses plan out the details until the last minute. That leads to situations like this:

Team: We need to order business cards for the new sales
  manager.

Manager: Cool, I'll find some online.

Looks through cheapest print options.

Manager: Wow, with this company, you only pay ship-
  ping and you get five hundred business cards for free!

*Ordered. The business cards arrive, and the print compa-
  ny's logo is on the back of each one. Congratulations,
  the company looks like it operates out of a garage.*

When you aren't intentional and you don't plan ahead,
you'll often choose the cheapest option instead of the best
one. Now, that isn't to say that the most expensive option is
always the right one. In fact, planning ahead often allows you
to stay within budgetary constraints while still integrating
excellence into your business. Often, last-minute decisions
are the most expensive decisions. And the options available
at the last minute are rarely good choices.

A little bit of planning on the front end will take your
guest experience to the next level and save you from future
headaches. Think through what the little details will communicate to your customer.

The benefits of forethought allow you to ensure you're
happy with what you communicate to your guests. And the
best way to do that is to storyboard your guest's experience
at your business. Walk through their approach scene by scene
(refer to chapter 5). Start with the big picture, then begin
integrating details into the whole experience. Walking in
the shoes of the guest helps you determine what you need to
communicate in each portion of the experience.

127

The Inconvenience of Intentionality

The problem with intentionality is that it's inconvenient for you. That's something you actually want to communicate to the guest, though. You want to communicate that you're willing to be inconvenienced in order to make a great experience for them.

JONATHAN

I always cringe whenever I see forms that have a section labeled "For Office Use Only." For many businesses, intake forms are one of their first points of contact with a guest. They're asking a first-time customer to trust them with their private information. But this simple "For Office Use Only" section tells them that this form is designed more for the administrative department than it is for the guest.

It indicates that the business wants to make it easy to process the guest's information—unintentionally telling the guest they are simply part of a process, not treated like a human being. Nobody wants to be processed. "For Office Use Only" is the type of thing you see on an IRS form. It isn't the type of thing you want on a form meant to mark the first connection your business has with a new customer.

Removing that "For Office Use Only" section from the form introduces inconvenience for the administrative office. There's no consistent place to mark that the form was processed and sent to the appropriate destination. It's a slight inconvenience. But a simple stamp on the back of the card or a sticky note could remedy that situation. It's more work, but it's worth it in order to communicate the correct thing to a new customer.

Anytime you approach something in your business—especially something for guests—with the mentality of "it's better for us internally," you're communicating something negative to the guest. If you're creating a hurdle for the guest because it's convenient for you, you won't like the results of what that says about you.

JASON

Recently I took my family to an amusement park. We were deep into the park when my wife turned to me and asked, "Did you get a map to show us where everything is?"

I hadn't. So I approached a park employee and asked if they had any available for us.

"No, sir, we don't have those here. Those are at the front of the park."

That created an immediate frustration. *You don't have them? What if someone forgets one like I did? What if their map gets wet? This amusement park is meant for families, yet you didn't anticipate the type of thing that commonly happens in a family situation?*

I made the lengthy trek back to the front of the park. The only maps available were in an area behind massive lines. In fact, I had to walk out of the main entrance to even find a map. I had to stand in the registration line even though I had already gotten into the park. The fact that they didn't provide maps around the park indicated to me that they were more concerned with not wasting paper than with providing a great experience for my family and me.

Would it have been wasteful to stock maps all around the park? Definitely. But that's an inconvenience that's worth the trouble for what it communicates to the guest.

When an organization is unwilling to inconvenience itself for the guest, there's a massive breakdown in the guest's experience. On the flip side, when an organization goes out of its way to do something for the guest, that creates a memorable moment.

JASON

I had a subscription to Birchbox for several years. It's a service that sends toiletries and beauty products to its subscribers each month for a small fee. One month, they left an item out of an order. I emailed them to let them know and asked that they send me the product.

Within an hour I received a response: "I'm so sorry. I sent it out today."

I was impressed with their quick recovery time. And they went on: "I'm also going to add 50 points to your account that you can use toward a purchase."

I never asked for that. I wouldn't have missed it if they hadn't offered it, because I simply wanted the product that had been left out. But that extra effort communicated that they understood my inconvenience. They chose to inconvenience themselves in order to make up for the extra trouble they caused me—little as it was.

Being intentional puts the extra effort on you. It inconveniences you to make a more memorable experience for the guest. And isn't that the way it should be? When you invite someone over to your house, you don't ask them to cook or to serve the food. You don't give them the uncomfortable chair while you sit on the luxurious couch. You go out of your way to care for them, and that communicates that they're valued and their comfort is more important than your own.

Communicating to the Senses

One of the things that made Sherlock Holmes such a brilliant detective was the way he relied upon all five senses to solve a case. He listened to the sounds. He smelled the scents. He touched the evidence. He might have even tasted a powder on the ground. He observed the nuances.

Human beings process through their five senses. When we talk about everything communicating, we must talk about *how* everything communicates. Your guests will "hear" you through their five senses. That means you'll communicate to them through what they see, hear, smell, touch, and taste.

Depending on your company, you probably focus on one or two of the senses through your product. If you're a restaurant, you're mostly concerned with taste, smell, and sight. If you're a dentist office, you're likely focusing on the senses of touch and sight, reducing the pain as much as possible and making the teeth look clean. If you're a hotel, you're focused on sights (decor), smells (cleanliness), and touch (the comfort of the beds).

Most businesses focus on the senses that are directly tied to their product, but they neglect the others. They do a disservice to their guest experience when they do that, because people remember things that are designed to tap into all the senses. Imagine building an experience that includes and considers everything sensory.

Abercrombie & Fitch stores capitalize on this idea. They've built an entire shopping experience based on the senses. You show up at the front of the store and are greeted by either a large, half-clothed model on a wall or a real-life, half-clothed model standing there. They pump their signature fragrance through the air-conditioning system, and their music is blasting loudly enough that you feel like you're already in the store before you've even breached the doors. The lighting, the music, the decor . . . they're all communicating something to your senses before you're even aware of the clothes. In fact, the clothes are almost an afterthought to the experience. Abercrombie & Fitch realizes they're selling an ideal more than an actual product.

While you might not be trying to manipulate impressionable teenagers, all businesses can learn a lot from that type of five-senses strategy. Consider what you might be communicating to your guests' senses.

Sight

The paint. The flooring. The carpets. The windows. The cleanliness. They all communicate something to your guests. Consider a restaurant. Most restaurants make sure the tables are clean, but we've all been to ones where we have to ask someone to wipe the table down before we eat. That communicates something.

What about dirty windowsills? Dingy bathrooms? Ceilings or decor with cobwebs visible?

On the other hand, what about bar stools or chairs that are angled out, seeming to invite the customer to sit down?

Sound

Does the volume of the music in your business match the level of energy in the room? If it's too quiet and the people in your business are animated and excited, it doesn't feel correct. If it's too loud and your older clientele can't even communicate with each other, it makes them want to leave. The type of music and the volume communicate something to a guest before they even interact with your product or service.

Unfortunately, we can't give you a specific soundtrack or decibel level for your business. That depends on your customer and the culture of your organization. If you're reaching young people, the music can be a bit louder with some edgy rhythms. But for older people, you might consider music that's a bit softer.

If a room has cool lighting and exciting prints on the walls, quiet Baroque-period music might seem a bit out of place. Or it might be so intentionally incongruous that it's cool.

Smell

JASON

One thing that always impresses me about Delta Sky Clubs is the smell they pump through their HVAC systems. It's a clean and classy smell, and it's intentional. They're trying to communicate a feeling to the guests who visit their airport lounges.

For some businesses, pumping a signature fragrance through the HVAC systems might seem over the top. But more simply, you can think about things like these:

- How do your restrooms smell? Do they smell like public restrooms at a sports stadium?
- What does your sales floor or lobby smell like? Fresh paint? Stale air? Does it smell pleasant?
- Do your team members have fresh breath?

The smells in your business are communicating.

Touch

What do your guests feel against their skin when they encounter your business? Are the fabrics of the chairs cheap? Does the paper of your brand material feel like copy paper—like it was just printed out of the back room instead of by a professional printer? What about the quality of toilet paper in the restrooms? Does it hurt your customer to have to take care of their basic needs? Each of those things is communicating something to your guest.

Taste

JONATHAN

My wife and I love to go to Miami once a year. She grew up there, and we both love Cuban food. We always make it a point to stay at a different hotel on Miami Beach—even choosing locations at South, Mid, or North Beach so we can have different experiences.

One of the things we love about visiting the hotels is the different infused waters they all have in their lobbies. Pretty much every hotel we've stayed at in Miami has water infused with cucumber, citrus, apple, pineapple . . . some mixture of fruit or vegetable to flavor the water. Those simple touches communicate things to us, and it has become almost a symbolic start to our vacation when we try the infused water our current hotel has to offer.

Even if your primary product isn't food related, there's probably some sort of taste element that happens at your business. Communicate excellence in that.

As you're planning the details of your business, think through ways you can communicate something more memorable through your guests' five senses. When you pay attention to these small details, you ultimately communicate to your guests that you value them. You communicate that you will take good care of them.

Key Points and Takeaways

1. Small details in your business communicate big things to your guest.

2. Being intentional with small details requires planning them ahead of time. The side benefit of planning ahead is that you often get a higher level of excellence for your business without paying a premium price.

3. Don't force other people into your way of doing things. Approach your systems from your guest's perspective, even if it means more inconvenience for you and your team.

4. Examine your guest's experience from the perspective of all five senses: sight, sound, smell, touch, and taste. Are the things that influence your guest's senses communicating excellence or a "taking shortcuts" mentality?

eight

Reject "Just Okay"

In 1988, Disney released a movie called *Who Framed Roger Rabbit?* It was a revolutionary mixture of live-action and animated characters—created in an era when modern special-effects technologies didn't exist. There's one scene from that movie that's famous in Disney's culture. The main character carries Roger Rabbit into a dark room, and in the process, he bumps a hanging lamp.

Of course, the live-action footage shows shadows dancing around the room. But this created a challenge for animators. Would they match those dancing shadows on their drawn rabbit? This would involve incredibly painstaking work. And at that time, when computer-generated special effects were still in their infancy, the audience probably wouldn't have even noticed Roger Rabbit's shadow. The standards for this type of special effect weren't high. The animators, though, decided it was worth their time to invest into the realism of the movie.

True, it was only one small part of a 104-minute movie. True, they could have gotten away with not adding the shadows and 99 percent of people wouldn't have noticed. But *they* would have known. And they were committed to making the movie excellent from beginning to end, even though this meant hours of extra work.

This scene birthed a phrase in Disney's culture: *bumping the lamp*. They refer to bumping the lamp any time they want to go the extra mile to make something excellent. Bumping the lamp means rejecting "just okay" and going above and beyond—even when it's possible nobody will notice the extra effort put into making something excellent.

Imagine if businesses put this type of effort into creating excellence for their guests. If a restaurant put this much attention into the cleanliness and experience of their restrooms. If a hotel cared about the smell of every room between the lobby and the guest's room. It would mean pursuing what is excellent even when it results in extra work that most people might not notice. That's what rejecting "just okay" is about. Excellence is doing the best you can, all the time. That means creating excellence for the guest during the first impression, the final impression, and every interaction in between.

The problem is, it's tempting to settle for "just okay." Businesses fall victim to this all the time. Over the years, our expectations for customer service have dropped. In fact, even when we get mediocre customer service, we often celebrate it by writing on a comment card. We've become so accustomed to bad service that "just okay" is often an improvement over the norm.

JONATHAN

Here's an example of a time I found myself celebrating "just okay" in a business situation. I recently got the privilege of flying first class on a four-hour flight. I wouldn't have paid the extra $800 for the seat, but I didn't mind taking it when they offered it to me for free.

As I boarded the plane before everyone else, I couldn't help but feel a bit smug as the other passengers watched. Yep, I was about to live the good life for the next four hours. I sat down in my comfortable leather seat (almost as comfortable as a La-Z-Boy), grabbed the headphones to enjoy an in-flight movie, and savored the beverage I was offered before the plane took off.

I pulled out my phone to snap a selfie, and as I was captioning my photo, the ludicrousness of the whole situation struck me. I thought this was the pinnacle of luxury—sitting in a reasonably comfortable seat with decent leg room and getting to enjoy a drink *before* taking off instead of in the air.

I realized I had become accustomed to what airlines have been able to offer the customer based on their price points, and I was celebrating as excellent service what I might expect on the ground to be the minimum. In former years, this was what people expected from an airline—whether in first class or coach. Mind you, that didn't keep me from enjoying the extra relaxation I got during that flight. But it reminded me of how easy it is to begin accepting "just okay."

Are you calling something first-class service that should be the bare minimum in your business?

Fortunately, this acceptance of mediocrity is starting to change. There are companies starting to reject the "just okay" mentality. Consequently, they're starting to magnify the weaknesses of brands that don't provide that level of service.

People are starting to notice areas where they became the frog in the boiling pot—where they slowly began accepting mediocre customer service from businesses they worked with.

This shouldn't be the reason your business chooses to reject "just okay." There's something more at stake here: your company's brand.

We aren't talking about the choice of logo, colors, and slogan. Those things are actually far less important than the reputation your company has. That's your true brand. When people think about your business, do they think about being cared for? Do they think about your attention to the details? Or do they think, *That company's just okay?*

How people feel after interacting with your company will be a far stronger determining factor on whether or not they come back than the best logo in the world. Your brand is what people feel when they think of you.

Where We're Tempted to Settle for "Just Okay"

There are five main areas in which it's tempting to settle for just okay—tempting for both you and your team. Let's explore these areas and see if you or your team has been in any of these situations.

1. When You Think People Won't See

It's tempting to do the bare minimum when you think nobody will see what you're doing. For example, a front-office team member at a doctor's office has her phone behind the desk, responding to a personal text message. There's no one in the waiting room. But then a guest cracks the door to the room and walks in silently. The team member is still looking down at her phone, and the guest waits there, unsure of what to do. Worse, the guest knows the team member is on her phone, not tapping away at a computer.

She assumed nobody would see, and she might never know that she missed an opportunity with a guest. That experience probably didn't ruin the guest's morning, but it certainly wasn't an excellent experience. If, instead, the team member had chosen to reject "just okay" in that moment when it appeared nobody would see her, the experience would have been excellent.

2. When Something Just Has to Get Done

JASON

Remember those mints I was so concerned about in our restrooms? We tried to keep them stocked. It was just a small thing we liked to provide, knowing it made the guest feel more confident about interacting with other guests. Those mints disappeared quickly based on the pace and volume of people who came through the building. One of the responsibilities of my team was to make sure the mint trays were filled all the time. It was a simple, even boring, task. But it was important to the team.

We also had a tray of mints in the lobby, but that one was almost always full because it was visible. The one in the bathroom was less visible to the team, so it became an out-of-sight, out-of-mind situation. That was one area where we always experienced the "just okay" principle. But it wasn't okay to me.

In fact, my fellow staff members figured out how much it annoyed me. If they saw an empty mint basket in the bathroom, they took a picture and sent it to me. They knew it drove me crazy. It became such a big joke among the team that I even got pictures when a staff member was out at a restaurant and noticed an empty mint basket. They captioned it, "Can you come fill this?"

It might just be a mint basket. It was just a task that needed to get done. But when our mint trays were full, it communicated to the guest that we were ready for them.

3. When You Don't Feel the Burden for Something

If you've ever been around someone in the military, you've probably heard the saying, "Close enough for government work." That's the sort of sentiment you hear when something simply *has to* be done and the person doing it doesn't feel the burden for it.

Whenever you stop feeling ownership for your role in serving guests, it's easy to accept "just okay." Sometimes a team member has never felt the burden to provide hospitality to the guest. (Is it up to the janitorial or housekeeping staff to do this? The kitchen staff? The stock team? The bank teller? Those in highly technical roles? Yes, it is.) Others used to have a burden, but it's faded. That's why it's important for leadership to consistently instill the vision of serving guests into the team.

When you don't feel the burden, you don't feel the responsibility of it. Then it becomes easy to assume that someone else will do what needs to be done, or that if it doesn't get done it isn't important enough anyway.

4. When It Feels Like the Stakes Are Lower

JASON

My family decided to go to a movie theater in the middle of the day. In the beginning of COVID-19, our school building was closed, so we had more flexibility in our day. And we live in Georgia, where some of the theaters were open.

If you've ever gone to a movie theater before 5:00 p.m., you know it's mostly deserted. They offer cheaper matinee showings because the crowd doesn't come until the evening.

It was clear the team felt that it wasn't important to keep the place clean. The theater was filthy. In an atmosphere where people are sensitive to sanitation and cleanliness, that made us worried. The theater advertised that they sanitized the seats between showings, but how could that be possible with messes on the floors?

The stakes were lower because the crowd was smaller, but I'll hesitate to return to that theater because of the experience my family had.

A guest should never get short-changed because the stakes seem lower.

- When it's 4:00 p.m., before the dinner rush, and there's only one person eating in the restaurant, it's easy to let things slide. (But someone's always looking.)
- When it's the off-season at a hotel and you're mostly just waiting around, it's easy to get distracted by personal calls or looking at memes on social media.
- When the construction contract is a small project that won't bring in as much money as large ones, it's easy to be worse at communicating and skip details

you might pay attention to if the project was a larger one.

5. When You Get Lazy

When you're lazy, either you've become too comfortable with the processes and you settle, or you've decided to cheat or cut corners one time. The problem is, you'll probably get away with it. But when one person cuts corners, others see it. Will they get away with it? Probably. Then another person chooses to cut corners one time and gets away with it. Then another.

Soon, one small action snowballs and spreads throughout the whole organization. Allowing "just okay" one time quickly becomes a license to allow it all the time.

We all feel lazy at times. That's normal. But a come back culture requires excellence even when we aren't feeling like it.

Always Improving

If you want to create a culture filled with people who "bump the lamp," you have to create an environment where you're always improving. The standard for excellence tomorrow should not be the same as it was yesterday. It should be raised incrementally each day.

In fact, that should be the number one reason you *don't* accept when people say, "We've always done it this way." If you've done something the same way for fifty years, that's an indication that you haven't improved in fifty years. Improvement requires processes to change.

Change doesn't have to be drastic, but it should be frequent. Each week should be slightly different than the week before. Sometimes you'll feel like you're taking a step back because you tried something new. That's okay. The true measure of excellence won't be found in one week. True excellence is a long-term move toward better processes and people, even if there are occasional deviations from that trend.

The process of always improving also involves letting multiple voices speak into a situation. Feedback is crucial because it's easy to stop seeing areas where improvement is possible. If you hope to institute a culture of constant improvement, it will require listening to these four voices that can help you improve your processes:

1. **Leadership.** If you're the leader, you naturally have the most at stake in creating a culture of constant improvement. You need to listen to yourself when it comes to new ideas on how to improve. If you aren't the leader, your desire to improve should come from a place of humility and service.

2. **Team members.** Team members are the front line. They hear stories and deal with the frustrations of the processes. A leader should ask their team at least annually for areas where they see potential for improvement.

   Or if you feel the burden for your team and want to be a great help to your leader, encourage your team members to talk to leadership when they see an area of improvement. Approach this with humility. Don't gang up on your leader and criticize. But do communicate areas where you feel things could be better. (Criticism is complaining; critique is offering a solution.)

3. **Guests.** Listen to guests. Don't rely on anecdotal evidence or singular stories, but look for consistently

mentioned items. Guests will tell you areas where you can improve through the things they avoid and through subtle things they say.

If you need to learn more from a guest, be sure you aren't defensive. Then listen and ask insightful questions to see what needs to change.

4. **Other department heads or managers.** (Even if they aren't part of your specific team.)

When we give permission for all four of those groups to speak into the process, we give people permission to create something more excellent. If you're the leader, the first voice is easy to listen to. But the last three can be a bit tougher. It will require humility on your part to listen to them—especially other team members. It requires pretty intense humility to be able to listen to your coworkers or those who work under you.

JASON

Many people get inspired by the show *Undercover Boss*. A high-powered CEO disguises themselves and walks among the ranks of their lower-level employees. They discover blind spots and hidden gems in their company.

Some find this inspiring, but I find it tragic. It means that the CEO has had the potential to improve and learn from mistakes all along, but there wasn't a system in place for feedback from team members or even guests.

How much better would it be if the CEO had an "always improving" mentality, had a humble approach, and looked for feedback from every part of their company?

Creating an atmosphere of ever-improving excellence requires that sort of humility and a "no sacred cows" approach
to evaluation. Everything should be on the table for feedback.
And feelings shouldn't get hurt when the feedback is given.

This requires an attitude of wanting to make the situation
better, instead of wanting to feel like you did a great job. The
sad truth is, constructive feedback will often make you feel like
a failure. When you enter into this process of finding places
where you can improve, you'll feel like you're doing nothing
right.

But you must remember that a few areas for improvement
don't undermine the many areas where you do your job well.
A squeaky wheel here and there will make the car seem like
it's falling apart. But it only indicates a few areas where
grease is needed. It's not the end of the vehicle.

Feedback is not an affront to your excellence. In fact, em-
bracing feedback will set a new bar for excellence.

When you get a customer review, embrace the feedback.
By leaving that review, the customer is actually creating a
vehicle for you to succeed. They actually want to show you
where you can improve. Resist the urge to become defensive
or to argue. In fact, come up with a plan to fix the situation
in the future and be willing to share it if you get a chance to
respond. That might be the "wow" that turns a customer
into a fan.

What Is Excellence?

If we must reject "just okay," what do we embrace instead?
What is this excellence we should be working toward? Excellence in a come back culture is:

- **Humble.** If you're full of pride, you won't be willing to listen to input. If you don't listen to input, you won't get the results of excellence.
- **Never-ending.** In any journey, there's an end goal. Unfortunately, in the pursuit of excellence, you'll never fully arrive. There's always a new pinnacle of greatness you can reach.
- **Relentlessly focused on continuous improvement.** If you lose your focus on improvement, you will always settle into a rhythm of autopilot. You'll become comfortable with processes, and you'll get sacred cows. Sacred cows are most often emotional—not actually sacred. They're things like:
  - processes that were set up by a personal hero
  - approaches you saw at a great company (just because it was right for them doesn't mean it is right for your company)
  - obtrusive or distracting decor that may hold sentimental value

  Sacred cows become untouchable assumptions that get in the way of forward progress.
- **Always thinking about culture.** If you aren't focused on maintaining a culture of excellence, you will always see a drift away from excellence. It is not the default. It has to be fought for. You must constantly ask yourself, "How can we enhance the team's culture? How can we make sure excellence stays part of our culture?"
- **Focused on both the guest *and* the team member.** Are you creating an excellent experience for both parties? Or are you focusing on the guest so much that you

neglect the team member who attends to the guest? A team member will generally treat the guest with the same care shown to them.

Consider an employee break room. Many of us have experienced the bleak spaces filled with artificial light, sterile (or worse, dirty) surfaces, and the mandated workforce posters displayed as the only decor. Those spaces can be anything but inspiring.

Now imagine the front of the business is beautifully decorated, welcoming, and warm, and the expectation is to provide incredible customer service. How would we expect a team member to walk out from that hideous space and be in the proper frame of mind to create an amazing experience for the guest? If a team member is uninspired behind the scenes, there's a good chance they'll be uninspired in front of people.

Compare that to a touring band. Whether they use their tour bus or a venue-provided greenroom, there's usually a comfortable space with dim lighting and relaxing chairs to help the band prepare before they go out on stage. Most break rooms, on the other hand, make the team member feel somewhat like a lab rat.

It's common for this to happen, but it shows lesser care to the people who are supposed to be delivering the care. And it inevitably begins to affect the way the team members interact with the guest. Where it's "just okay" to create a drab break room for the employee, it becomes "just okay" to provide subpar care for the guest.

"Just okay" seems harmless, but it is a virus that will infect your whole organization if you leave it unchecked. In order for excellence to become the standard, it has to be valued in every single corner and crevice of the business.

There are five areas where you have the opportunity to create excellence for your guests or simply accept "just okay":

1. **The leader.** Even leaders can be guilty of settling for "just okay." If you're facing a season of burnout, it might be time to take a break so you can regain your passion once again. If you've lost the burden, maybe it's time to remind yourself why you got into your industry in the first place.

2. **The team member.** Perhaps the team member needs a reminder of the impact they have. Because of who they are—the way they look, act, dress, smile, talk—their welcoming demeanor can create an experience for the guest that no one else can.

3. **The processes.** The training might be lacking or the tools for recovery might be missing. Maybe it's time to schedule a training time or bring in an outside perspective to refresh the processes.

4. **The culture (internal).** A guest will feel what the team member feels. If a team member feels that the culture is one of settling, the guest will feel that too. Reach out to staff and get their honest perspective on the culture of the business. Working on the inside (your culture) influences the impact on others.

5. **The brand (external).** When a guest interacts with team members, they are interacting with the brand. If they perceive the team member as excellent, they will tend to perceive the brand as excellent. If the team

member perceives the brand as excellent, they will tend to provide extra excellence. It's a self-fulfilling prophecy. Give the team member a reputation to be proud of, and you'll find they live up to that reputation.

Do people perceive your business as excellent? Do they perceive your check-in system as excellent? The front-desk team member? The cleaning crew? The payment processing? The support? Or is your business's brand one of mediocrity?

As you seek to reject "just okay" in your business and reach for excellence, ask yourself the following three questions. Apply them to those five areas. Then keep asking these questions as you continue to improve your people and your processes.

1. **What's worth starting?** Should you implement a new process or find new tools to help you achieve excellence in a come back culture?
2. **What's worth fixing?** Is there a process that isn't functioning properly that merely needs a tweak or a reorganization to make it work the way it was meant to?
3. **What's worth ending?** If there is something distracting from excellence, it's important to stop it. Is there a policy that gets in the way of your team members providing excellent care? Is there something unnecessary that's done in a mediocre way that your team would be better off not doing?

Excellence is not easy. It's inconvenient. But the work is worth it to make your brand synonymous with excellence.

Key Points and Takeaways

1. Excellence is doing the best you can, all the time, even when you think no one will notice.

2. Many of the people visiting your business are getting their first glimpse of your brand. Will that glimpse be of excellence or of mediocrity?

3. The standard for excellence tomorrow should not be the same as it was yesterday. If you're doing some things because you've always done them that way, it means you haven't been improving in those areas.

4. An atmosphere of continuing excellence requires a "no sacred cows" approach, where everything in your business is up for discussion and improvement.

5. Three questions will help you find areas where you can improve: What's worth starting? What's worth fixing? What's worth ending? There are some things—even good things—that you should stop doing if they aren't pushing your organization toward excellence.

nine

Choose Values over Policies

JASON

Daniel works live events at his organization, serving in the parking lots. He is intentionally placed in the parking lot where parents park. If you knew Daniel, you'd know why.

Each time you approach the parking lot, you'll find Daniel wearing a lime-green vest and waving two light sabers (aka orange light wands) while safely parking cars and helping people walk into the building. The thing that sets Daniel apart isn't necessarily his excellence at performing the task—though he *is* excellent. What sets him apart is his fun dance moves. He gets into it each time he works and has so much fun dancing that guests can't help but smile as they find their parking space.

Daniel takes potentially aggravated parents—dealing with the stress of parking lots and preschoolers complaining in the minivan—and creates a great experience for them. His decision to let his personality shine creates a positive vacation from stress for everyone. In addition, it sends a small message that he loves what he does.

153

This is a visible embodiment of one of the values of his organization: the value of having fun.

Values, principles, priorities—whatever you want to call them—are far more important than policies, because they evoke responses from team members that you can't manufacture. For instance, you could try to tell your parking lot attendants to dance. But for many, it would seem mechanical or uncomfortable. In Daniel's situation, the "having fun" value allowed him to highlight his unique personality to create a one-of-a-kind experience. For another volunteer, this value might mean juggling or telling quick jokes to people when appropriate. For still another, it might just mean smiling because they truly enjoy their role.

Values are our filters that help us make decisions as an organization. They're ideas, behaviors, and truths we embrace that determine what we do or don't do. Values tell our team members what matters most. When we establish a set of values for our team, we are declaring the important elements of what we believe so we can do what matters. *This is why we do what we do.*

The power in values-driven business is that it makes decisions easy for staff members. When a situation or question arises, the team member doesn't have to scroll through a list of policies in their mind or refer to a manual. They can simply reflect back on their organization's values and see whether or not an action aligns with them. *We value having fun in this organization, so how should I respond to this situation in a way that reinforces that value yet doesn't make the guest feel uncomfortable?*

The truth is, it's impossible to have policies in place that cover every situation. Unexpected things always happen. Hospitality happens in the way you deal with the unexpected.

Think of it like this: Whenever new technology arises, governments have to determine whether they should create new laws to regulate the use of it. Consider cell phones in cars. A few years ago, many cities made laws to keep people from talking on their phones while driving. Recently many cities added texting to the list of banned activities. But what about when new technology arises that potentially distracts a driver? What about using the GPS on their phone? What about new head-up-display technologies? Virtual reality?

When you are a policy-driven organization, you have to make new rules each time a situation arises. In many cases, companies make rules before anything even happens, just in case. But in a values-driven organization, the values don't change. The applications change.

In the situation of cell phones in cars, you could keep making policies:

- Don't reroute your GPS while the car is in motion.
- No using virtual reality headsets while driving, unless the field of vision is at least 120 degrees.
- No applying makeup while the car is in motion.

The list of laws would become ridiculous, because situations keep changing.

Or you could simply say, "As a nation, we value distraction-free driving. Don't drive distracted." That covers texting, phone calls, reading your mail, applying makeup . . . the gamut. For each person, the value manifests itself in different

155

actions and different ways. But one simple value makes it easy to decide. *Will I be distracted by performing this activity? Then I won't do it.* The value covers thousands of different potential situations, and it takes the guesswork out of them.

Obviously, values-driven systems don't necessarily work well for governments. But in an organization that is carefully crafting training and culture, values can help steer team members without the need for a fifty-page manual filled with policies for every potential situation.

Why should your organization be run by values instead of policies?

- Values last. They aren't created at the whim of trends.
- Values keep you from having lists of constrictive rules. They provide freedom for individuality.
- Values help make things consistent across the organization.

Here are the questions for your business: Do you have a list of values? Does your team know the values? Do they know what to do with them? Values should be basic, but they are remarkable when integrated into the behaviors of the organization.

You can coach new team members from the values. You can let people go if they don't adhere to the values. You can know what you do as an organization, and you can know what you *don't* do as an organization.

Many organizations have a list of values, but if those values don't permeate everything the organizations do, they're simply nice statements. For instance, if you're pleased with something someone does that contradicts one of your organization's values, your values aren't real values. Or if someone gets in trouble for doing something that aligns with one of your business's values, again, your values aren't real values.

Think of a waitress at a restaurant. She's laughing with her customers, engaging them in conversation, and having a great time. If the organization values having fun but a manager gets upset at her for doing that, it shows that it's not truly a value of the organization. The manager might even be upset that the waitress isn't seeing other tables quickly enough, but if he doesn't acknowledge that she's accomplishing one of the values of the organization before encouraging her to speed up her service, it creates a dissonance between what the company says and what it celebrates.

This type of thing creates an unstable culture for an organization. People don't really know what will make the leader or team members happy because whims seem to dictate proper behavior instead of values upon which everyone can agree.

It's important to have a short list of values—three or four—that can bring everyone onto the same page when it comes to serving guests. They should be simple enough that people can remember them and actually do something about them.

Identifying the Values

JASON

I once worked at a church where attendance usually exceeded seven thousand people each Sunday, and we created a great set of values for the guest services team. They had four values: (1) show care, (2) have fun, (3) remain flexible, and (4) deliver wow.

The guest services team members especially excelled at value #3 (remain flexible). Depending on the weekend schedule and the season of attendance, the guest flow varied. Therefore, they paid attention to where the guest needed them—not necessarily where "my spot" was.

There was a lady who volunteered there who understood this need. She started out in one spot, moved to another, and then switched again to a different position, all within 150 feet of where she originally started. She did all of this in one hour. Why? She paid attention to where people were going and identified the optimal place for her to stand to help the guest feel the benefit. She was not focused on always being in the same spot each week. Her approach was, "I'll go where I'm needed, and while there, I will be flexible to respond to the flow and needs of people."

If a volunteer can do this, imagine how much more a paid team member could do!

That church allowed the four values to direct everything their guest services team did. But your business's values might look a little different. Your value statements need to reflect what matters to your organization, to your leadership, and to the customers you're trying to reach.

Different organizations use different methods to arrive at their list of values: online assessments, decks of cards that list different values, exploring what matters to the company, uncovering what matters to the leader . . . There are many different ways to discover your values, but one of the easiest ways is simply to work through some questions. For instance, if you're the leader, start by creating a personal list of values for your family or life. You might work through questions like these:

- What makes me come alive?
- What makes me feel bad?
- What makes me happy?
- What makes me mad or sad?
- Where have I failed?
- What was it about that failure that made me still come alive and move forward?
- Where have I seen the greatest amount of movement or results?
- When people compliment me or critique me, what do I hear?
- What books do I read the most?
- What things keep me up at night?
- What things are natural for me?
- What are things I've learned from family members?

Then you simply combine those things into a list of words or phrases that reflect your personal values. Next, process those values with what your organization values.

- What matters to the company already?
- What does the team already do well?
- What do we already do for the guest?
- What things do we intentionally *not* do for the guest?
- What might the guest know they want?

- What might the guest want but not know they want?
- What can we do to make the guest feel comfortable, safe, etc.?
- What are the basic needs of a guest?
- Why does a team member want to be part of the team?
- What must happen in our environment that contributes to a remarkable experience?

Then put those things into words and combine your lists. Although you want the values to primarily reflect your organization, the value list you adopt for your team will probably reflect your personality and goals because you're part of the team. If you're a leader, any team will tend to reflect your personality to a small degree, because that's what leadership does—it leaves its fingerprint on things.

Finally, begin pruning, combining, and removing from the list. Some of the values will be similar, so combine them. Some of them will seem like good ideas but aren't actually true values for your team or organization. Finally, some of them will be behaviors, not values. You can save behaviors for later; you don't want to include them in your list of values.

Work through these and begin incorporating them into your team.

If your company has branches in diverse locations, there's a good chance they will have slightly different approaches when it comes to serving the guest. Local cultures will value different things—think lower-income rural versus higher-income urban. Also consider your guest's psychographic variables. Changing the way you operate to match local values won't mean a reduction in excellence but a change in how your team operates.

What about if you're a team member and your leader hasn't established a list of values? The good news is, you can still figure out your leader's values and implement them in your personal approach to serving guests. You can explore the policies already in place, then ask yourself why they exist. (Sometimes this can be difficult if certain policies have been inherited from previous leaders.) Explore the spirit of the rule; that's where you'll find the real value behind the policy.

Even if a leader hasn't verbalized their values, they still have them. They just haven't thought about them yet. You can, with humility, walk your leader through this process and help them discover their own values. Yes, you can revolutionize your team even if you aren't in a leadership position.

Integrating the Values

JONATHAN

I was eating at a restaurant with a friend who had brought his three-year-old daughter with him. The waitress approached our table and took our drink orders. My friend asked if they had a kids' menu available, and the waitress, annoyed, left to grab one. When she came back, she apologized because they were out of crayons for the toddler to color on the menu.

My friend spoke up. "Observation: You've been out of crayons the last two times I came here."

Of course, everyone at the table shrank in embarrassment because of my friend's rude approach to the waitress. But I noticed that he had picked up on something. The restaurant had designed a special kids' menu and even decorated areas to try to make kids love eating there. But simple things like consistently not having crayons on hand showed that they hadn't fully integrated the value of being kid-friendly.

It's important to empower the team to act out your business's values. Something to be able to impress the parents' kids is a great way to reinforce a value of kid-friendliness.

Whenever you set a list of values for your team, behaviors need to follow. If they don't, you've simply created a nice list of phrases that will live on a wall somewhere until some archeologist digs it up in the distant future.

So how do you go from a list of platitudes to an active, breathing list of values that affects everything your team does? Here are ten steps to help leaders turn their values into a reality.

1. Live out the values.

If one of your values is to have fun, the leader needs to set the tone for that. It's nearly impossible for someone to have fun when their leadership is stressed out. If you're the leader, create a fun environment for your team. Laugh with them. Don't stress out when someone shows up late. Don't ice people out if they're unavailable when you need them. Model the behavior you're trying to see in your team.

As the team sees their leader living out the values, they'll follow along.

2. Teach the values.

Great leaders teach their values to their team and teach them often. It's been said, "Repetition is the price of knowledge." It often takes at least three times for someone to hear something before they actually understand what they're hearing.

Teach the values in different ways. Some people are auditory learners, meaning they need to hear what's being taught. Some are visual, meaning they need to see it. Still others are kinesthetic, meaning they need to participate in the learning process. Present the values in different ways each time you teach them so you can make sure everyone catches them. You might even consider printing out a gigantic, beautiful poster with the values and plastering it on the walls of the staff room. It's actually better if it's a temporary fixture on the wall; people tend to ignore permanent fixtures after a week or two.

3. Acknowledge the values when you see them in team members.

People place value on the things you praise. Make sure you're praising the correct things.

For instance, if parents raise a young daughter always telling her how beautiful she is, that child will grow up believing beauty is of utmost importance. She'll believe that being beautiful is the way to make people happy with her. Thus her life will center on beauty. However, if her parents instead praised things like integrity, honesty, and bravery, those would become the focus of her life—even into adulthood.

While you might not have the same impact on your team members as a parent raising a young child, your praise will ultimately determine what your team values, even if you aren't the leader. When you praise a team member for embodying one of your team's values, others will see it and naturally adopt that same value in their own conduct.

4. Identify creative and memorable ways to communicate the values.

One of the habits of great leaders is the ability to communicate using stories. Malcolm Gladwell, Seth Godin, and even politicians all use stories in compelling ways to make their point. Politicians will even bring people to their debates as visual aids to make their stories seem more personal. There's something about stories and the unexpected that sticks in our minds. Use these story devices to make your values memorable for your team.

If you're the leader, you might even consider empowering your team to brag on their fellow team members in a meeting: "How have you seen a team member demonstrate these values?" Highlight and celebrate those wins that reinforce your values.

5. Select people for the team who already live out the values.

When it comes to hiring processes, look for and select employees who already demonstrate your values. In fact, you might craft interview questions about ways they would respond to certain situations. If they would respond in manners consistent with your company's values, there's a good chance they would be a great fit for your team. And if they feel like a great fit, their work will be better. This might be even more important than résumé competencies!

Plus, if you're starting from scratch with a new set of values, these new team members can become great examples for the team. You can refer to them in moments of teaching or encourage them to challenge their teammates to do what they do.

6. Create ways for team members to participate in the values.

Empower your team to do things that support the values. For instance, simple activities for kids might make it easy for a waiter to provide a great experience for them. As you train your team and make these types of tools available, you're further reinforcing your belief in the values. Plus you make the values tangible with a specific way they can be turned into a behavior.

7. Talk with team members about what happens when values don't go well.

Just like you want to paint a vision of what could happen when the values work in conjunction with behavior, explain what can happen when they don't work. Personalize the stories you tell. Chances are, most of your team members will be able to empathize with a story you tell; we've all been victims of poor customer service.

8. Attach behaviors to each value.

This is where you can bring back the list of behaviors you removed when you were making your list of values. Under each value, make a list of supporting behaviors.

JASON

The guest services values at the church from earlier in this chapter had supporting behaviors that looked like this:

165

- Show Care
  - Anticipate and fulfill needs.
  - Acknowledge each person.
  - Intentionally listen and respond appropriately.
  - Give a warm greeting and goodbye.
- Have Fun
  - Share a smile.
  - Have a joyful attitude.
  - Show elements of your personality.
  - Keep interactions upbeat and positive.
- Remain Flexible
  - Provide quick service recovery.
  - Find a gap and fill it.
  - Support each other.
  - Use autonomy inside the framework to problem-solve.
- Deliver Wow
  - Do little things really well.
  - Make personal connections with people.
  - Create surprise-and-delight moments.
  - Think through nonverbal gestures.

9. *Give and receive feedback through the filter of the values.*

Something will go wrong. You can expect that. When it does, as much as possible, tie the error back to the values. "What happened today wasn't a good example of *showing care.* Here's how we could have done things differently." Behaviors are much easier to correct when you show people the why behind the desired behavior. Your values are the why.

10. *Give team members incremental steps on aligning with the values.*

Never criticize a team member who's misaligned with the values. In *How to Win Friends and Influence People*, Dale Carnegie suggests this: "Use encouragement. Make the fault seem easy to correct."[1] When you provide simple, tangible steps of improvement to a team member, it gives them something to aim for. Nobody wants to feel like a situation is hopeless. Give them hope that they can fit into the team, and show them how to do it.

Keeping the Values Alive

Once you've integrated your values into your business, revisit them often. Don't let them become just another mission statement or vision statement that sits on a plaque or a paper only to collect dust. Filter every single thing your team does through these values and keep them fresh for your organization. That will mean dropping some behaviors that don't align with the values. It will also mean tweaking the values to align with some of the behaviors you want to see happen in the team.

JASON

After a training session, one of my new team leaders approached me and said, "You really believe all this, don't you? You believe the four values you shared can guide what we do and make us successful."

I do.

My passion for these values translated to that leader. He saw that I really meant what I was saying. And that translated to his team. When we value the values, our team does too. They'll see your passion, they'll catch it, and the values will spread.

⸺⸺

You'll know your team members have internalized the values when they start coming up with their own creative ideas: "I know one of our values is 'have fun,' so I thought it would be a great idea to give our event teams colorful signs that say things like 'Welcome,' 'Looking good today,' 'So glad you're here,' and so on." When your team members surprise you with new ideas that reinforce your organization's values, you'll know they value the values.

They'll also be quick to point out policies that conflict with the values. If you're a leader, be willing to hear those critiques and make changes when necessary. You can't allow policies to win over values.

Key Points and Takeaways

1. Policy-driven organizations have to make new rules each time a situation arises. Values-driven organizations, on the other hand, can help steer team members without having to create a fifty-page manual filled with policies for every potential situation.

2. Your real values won't necessarily match your written values. Real values are the things you praise and the things you build habits around to create disciplines that get results.

3. Values are different from behaviors. But a great statement of supporting behaviors can help cast the vision for your values.

4. There are ten great ways to integrate your values into your organization.

   a. Live out the values.

   b. Teach the values.

   c. Acknowledge the values when you see them in team members.

   d. Identify creative and memorable ways to communicate the values.

   e. Select people for the team who already live out the values.

   f. Create ways for team members to participate in the values.

   g. Talk with team members about what happens when values don't go well.

   h. Attach behaviors to each value.

   i. Give and receive feedback through the filter of the values.

   j. Give team members incremental steps on aligning with the values.

ten

Build a Hospitable Team

JASON

I took my daughter to a casual Italian restaurant for Valentine's Day. It is a national chain not known for their remarkable service. But the experience we had was remarkable—so much so that my daughter was talking about it for days after.

The waitress approached our table and was remarkable from the beginning. She was friendly, and it was clear my daughter related to her. There was a certain aspirational element about the waitress's personality that inspired admiration in my daughter.

We both wanted soup, so we asked the waitress to list the options. My daughter immediately knew which soup she wanted, but I had a harder time making a decision. I told the waitress that three were off the table, but I couldn't decide between two.

"I tell you what," she said. "I'll bring you bowls of both and you can tell me which one you like."

"Are you sure?" I said. "I don't want to get you in trouble."

"I got you," she said.

I was surprised, because that wasn't the normal approach to ordering. Most servers get annoyed that you're having difficulty deciding; after all, they have other tables to serve. But she not only didn't force me into a decision, she gave me full control. She crafted a personal and customizable experience inside the bigger restaurant experience. She wins the award for creating a remarkable experience, and it's a moment that I want to remark about to others.

You'll notice that in this story, the waitress didn't say, "I need to check with _____." If she had, it wouldn't have made the experience remarkable. "I need to check with _____" is the type of approach to customer service that car dealers employ. It wears a customer down. It shows distrust and sometimes even hostility among the team members and with the customer.

Instead, the waitress took control of the situation with full confidence. That indicated there was plenty of trust:

- *Trust with her manager.* She knew she wouldn't get in trouble for the extra.
- *Trust with the kitchen staff.* They wouldn't get mad at her for making more work for them.
- *Trust with the customer.* She wasn't skeptical that I was trying to take advantage of her.

This story is an indication of a team that trusts each other, which is an indication of a team that shows hospitality to each other.

The truth is, if you don't feel hospitality among your team members, you won't be able to demonstrate it to the customer. Internal hospitality enables external hospitality. When a team gathers together with the unified goal of helping the customer, they succeed.

It isn't a case of managers versus employees, or making money versus doing what the customer wants. A team that shows hospitality to each other is a team built on trust.

The question is, how do you build trust and hospitality into your team? There are four measures of a hospitable team:

- Assuming the best
- Befriending each other
- Learning from and teaching others
- Encouraging others

We'll explore those four elements in the rest of this chapter. If they're present, you'll find you have a hospitable team. If they aren't, there are some things you can do to change that.

Assuming the Best

When it comes to power and communication, there are a lot of opportunities for assumptions. Why did the president make the decision he did? Was it for the reason he said, or was there some other political purpose he was hiding behind his action?

Why did my leader choose that word? Was there something deeper hidden in what she was saying? Was she being passive-aggressive? Was she trying to keep me from learning the truth?

Why did my coworker tell that to my leader? Was he trying to get our team in trouble? Is he angling for a promotion by stepping all over his coworkers?

We've all experienced people with hidden agendas. It starts with parents or siblings. Then it moves on to classmates or teachers. And eventually we see it happen in the workplace. Assuming the best might have come naturally to us at birth, but countless interactions have beat it out of us. Many of us have a healthy skepticism about people's motives. (Some have become overly skeptical and find it difficult to trust anyone.)

The problem is that a team filled with skeptics isn't able to provide excellent hospitality. They'll always assume that the guest is trying to take advantage of them. Or that they'll get in trouble if they make a mistake and help the customer too much. Or that a coworker will make fun of them if they go above and beyond the call of duty.

Great hospitality requires some vulnerability when it comes to shielding the guest from negative experiences, and people aren't willing to be vulnerable on a team unless they trust their team members.

JASON

I once worked with a client that was experiencing rapid growth and had a long history of success. As I began to interact with a few of their key leaders, I accidentally stumbled onto an element that employees were not publicly talking about but whose impact they were privately feeling almost daily.

An executive in the organization had been hired to bring order and to enable the C-suite to focus on areas where they could make the greatest impact. His energy, his skills at rallying everyone together, and his quick decision-making ability became an instant help.

However, as time progressed, what was a strength in the beginning became a clog in the system. In fact, this leader thought highly of his ability to carry a lot of responsibilities and make fast decisions. Eventually, quick decisions slowed down, stopped being made at all, or worse, were made when they were advantageous to the leader. Needless to say, certainty about direction and clarity about roles were rare. Employees started to ask themselves if they wanted to remain employed with this organization.

What was the greatest violation? Trust had been breached by the executive, and now other team member relationships were bruised by diminishing trust. On top of it all, the culture was not safe to demonstrate vulnerability by asking questions or challenging what felt unhealthy. Therefore, trust ran thin.

There was one specific area where I noticed this trust issue the most. Intentional care and remarkable attention toward guests started to fade. This was shown in the way team members spoke to guests, overlooked guests, and prioritized their own preferences over what created a memorable and meaningful guest experience. As I began to ask their leaders strategic questions, the team began to realize and embrace the challenge of repairing what was broken. They collectively made the intentional decision to focus on team emotional safety, which requires vulnerability, and trust has increased as a result.

As of this writing, the team has made improvements, and this is reflecting positively in the guest experience. The organization realized that the dysfunction and unhealthiness inside the house finds its way to the porch and yard. In other words, what happens inside can eventually be seen and felt by those outside the day-to-day operations.

If you've noticed a culture of distrust in your organization, you need to fix it. And the first step to fixing it comes from the top.

As a leader, what decisions have you made lately? Did they make your team members feel supported, or did they make them feel isolated? Have you celebrated wins? Have you celebrated when people took initiative, even if it led to a failure? Have you done a good job at communicating the reason behind decisions your team members might not agree with?

A pattern of support is one of the first ways to remedy a team that assumes the worst about leadership. Next, though, you need to ensure there are no gaps in communication.

A gap in communication is simply the space where people can fill in their own information. It's when communication is incomplete, leaving room for people to come up with their own conclusions. Gaps most often arise when people are afraid to ask questions or when there isn't an opportunity for questions to be asked.

This is seen most often when senior leadership makes a decision, then midlevel management is called in to implement that decision. Lower-level employees might have questions that midlevel managers aren't equipped to answer, and assumptions grow. It's important to create a system where people can get answers to their questions so as to avoid creating a culture of assuming the worst. Remember that when gaps exist, they get filled with information, and it's often wrong information.

Is there a direct line of communication between the decision makers and those affected by the decisions? Are questions encouraged?

Square, a payment-processing company, has built a company policy to combat these gaps in communication. Every decision made at the company—an organization with over six hundred employees—is public knowledge within the company. If two or more people gather for a meeting, someone has to take notes and post them where the whole company can review them. This even applies to board meetings.[1]

It's hard for people to make assumptions when they can just look at the notes from the meetings. *Was someone trying to take advantage of me? I'll just read the notes. Did they consider _____? I'll read the notes.*

This type of approach might not work at every company, but you can borrow the heart behind it. Transparency and a healthy feedback loop can create a culture where your team can assume the best of each other.

Befriending Each Other

We've all seen unhealthy workplace friendships develop. In fact, movies are made about this stuff.

At a restaurant, there's that one guy who seems to date all the servers. Then the drama we know and love from teen rom-com movies ensues. Someone quits their job because they can't deal with the drama. Still another plays pranks on the guy, trying to get even with him. A couple of others join forces and do something else. Then you have the manager looking at all the chaos, trying to figure out what happened. And customers have received poor service and even heard hostility in team members' voices.

Because of this nightmare scenario, it's tempting to try to keep a workplace so professional that there's no opportunity for friendship. Just like the toxic closeness from our example creates a horrible experience for the guest, a workplace that feels cold and distant can create the same type of experience.

It's good to have boundaries for your team, but they shouldn't come at the expense of colleagues who enjoy working together. Coworkers can accomplish much, but friends can accomplish even more. Coworkers tend to do their part in the process and leave the rest alone. But friends will make up for areas where their friends are falling short. They'll protect and cover for each other, creating a safe environment of trust.

If you need to set some boundaries because your workplace has become toxic, do that. Find the source of the unhealthy drama and make some changes. Firing might be necessary.

But if you find your workplace is experiencing the opposite situation—coldness, distance, and indifference—it's time to do some things to foster a sense of friendship and community. You should see your team members joking with each other, grabbing a drink at the end of the day, and being able to rely on one another.

Here are some ways to foster that sense of friendship and community.

Shared Vocabulary

It's a natural thing for groups to create their own shared vocabulary. You see it in athletics, education, community groups . . . It's almost like a password challenge: if you respond with the right verbiage, it shows you're authorized to be in the group. You're one of them.

The best shared vocabulary should be familiar, intentional, and mission focused. Referring to customers as "guests" is one perfect example.

You might even take it a step further and refer to customers like pop stars refer to their fans. You have Beliebers for Justin Bieber, Arianators for Ariana Grande, and Swifties for Taylor Swift. You can create a special name for your superfans: _____ Nation or _____ Fans. Gauge this by the culture of your team. If the culture is one of exaggeration and fun, this might be a great approach. If it's more corporate and professional, this might be a step too far and might not match the mission of your organization.

Nicknames

There's something about a nickname that makes people feel like they belong. Assuming it's not a name they hate, a nickname makes them feel like they have a custom role in the group. And if it's one that's customized for the team, it can create an instant sense of belonging and camaraderie.

Just make sure the nickname comes from a place of celebration and don't try to force it. Instead, look for something a team member does well or a time they did something remarkable. Give them a name that reinforces their value on the team.

Celebrating Together

Look for an opportunity to celebrate with your team. Especially if your team has gone through a particularly busy season, create a party to commemorate the fact that everyone survived. Better yet, look for any small opportunity to celebrate. This could be a party, a special snack, or a commemorative T-shirt.

There's a classic Southwest Airlines joke that shows how well the company celebrates:

> How many Southwest employees does it take to change a light bulb?
>
> Four—one to change the bulb and three to make the T-shirt.[2]

If celebration becomes a large part of your culture, you'll find customers joking about it. That's a good thing, because yet again it's a shared experience.

You can also plan extra events off-campus to celebrate. Here are some ideas:

- bowling
- Topgolf
- a cookout in a manager's backyard or a park
- a carnival or fair
- a movie night
- an escape room
- hiking
- a cooking class

Shared Points of Connection

Finally, look for areas of commonality among your team. Are there any new parents? Strike up a conversation with them. Make it natural; don't just call them into an office and try to force them to play with each other. Sometimes friendships just need a gentle nudge to get them started.

You can't force friendship. There will be some who will always clock in and clock out at their job without making lasting connections with their coworkers. That's okay. People have busy lives. But if you create a culture of camaraderie and connection at your organization, you'll find that culture making its way into the guest experience.

Learning from and Teaching Others

JONATHAN

I worked in a creative director role quite a few years ago. It was in the city where I met and married my wife. When she had the opportunity to go to physical therapy school in another city, I had a specific timeline for when my role at the organization would end. I gave my boss a five-month notice.

The role was a high-level one. A lot of the creative expression of the organization centered on my ideas, my methods, and the things I did. Those five months were valuable in training others and sharing my knowledge.

Let me tell you, that was one of the most freeing five months for me. I no longer worried that I would become obsolete. I no longer worried someone would replace me. I was *trying* to replace myself. I can say that the organization took huge steps forward during that time because there was a sense of learning from and teaching others in my department. I actually wished I would have taken that approach earlier on in my career. The reason I didn't, though, was because a person's value to the organization was what they could provide in a given moment. If they weren't the best person for the job, they weren't the person for the job.

———

There are a couple reasons your team members might not be focusing on learning from and teaching others. First, it takes effort. And second, there's a real fear that if someone comes along who can do the team member's job better than them, they'll no longer have a role in the organization. This is true even at lower levels of an organization. Most often, managers and leaders celebrate someone who is exceptional in their role. We celebrate the game-winning basket; we don't celebrate the team members who taught a specific skill to the person who made that basket. And we often overlook the team member who might not reach their full potential as a basketball player because they spend their time investing in other team members.

What would happen to someone in your organization who passed on all their knowledge to so many people that they worked themselves out of a job?

Ideally, you'd move them to a position of management, because they've shown aptitude in empowering others. But are your employees aware that this is in their future? Or have they seen others who might be rock stars in their roles but are not necessarily team players being celebrated?

It's important to celebrate the sharing of knowledge.

In business, we love talking about trade secrets. They're our unique approaches or technologies that give us a competitive advantage over other organizations. They're a valuable distinguisher between organizations. However, many companies have trade secrets within their own ranks. Formulas, processes, information—there are employees who want to keep those to themselves so they don't lose their competitive advantage over their coworkers.

Trade secrets shouldn't exist within an organization. The team should never fall apart because someone unexpectedly got sick or went on maternity leave or had to move to another city. This type of approach obviously affects the quality of the product or service your company offers. But it's also reflective of competition, where the customer merely becomes a tool for someone to get ahead.

This is one reason some organizations rotate competencies. Sometimes you work in one role and other times you work in another role. That's one valid approach, but for organizations that work with high specialization or require specific competencies, that isn't much of an option.

For those situations, you might institute a shadowing rotation, where employees get paid for extra training to follow a coworker around for a day when they don't need to perform their role. The goal is not to hand off responsibilities but to help create empathy for others' roles and to promote learning. Who knows whether an innovation in one role might become a useful innovation in another?

Another way you could approach this is encouraging team members to prepare TED Talk–like lessons about something unique they're doing in their role. Have them present those to the whole organization.

As you show that sharing knowledge is important to the culture of your organization, you'll see it happen more often. This helps break down silos between departments, but it also creates a sense of trust among the team. Reward those who learn and those who share with others, and you'll see the hospitality level of your team rise. And that hospitality extends to the customer.

Encouraging Others

Have you ever worked in a role where you weren't sure whether your boss thought you were doing a good job? You knew you were getting your tasks done effectively, but you weren't sure what your boss thought. Were they pleased with your results? Were they happy with *you* being in that role?

Here's the thing: We want to be good at the things we do. It's the reason we have hobbies—we want fulfillment in something we're interested in, and we want to be good at it.

It's also the reason some teenagers rebel against strict parents. If they grow up feeling overly criticized, like they can never make their parents happy, they'll sometimes swing to the opposite extreme and do things to intentionally displease their parents.

Can we make a bold prediction? Much of the laziness or indifference an organization might experience from its employees comes from those who think they can't do a good job, so they stop trying.

It might not even be the fault of a manager that an employee feels that way. Of course, our societal approach to authority makes us look to our leader first for affirmation in our role, but our natural wiring toward community makes us also look to our peers. We want those around us to see our value.

If an employee feels insecure in their value, either with their leader or with their peers, they have one of two approaches:

- They intentionally don't try, or they show indifference so nobody can accuse them of failing since they never were trying to succeed in the first place.
- They try to grab credit for good things or shift blame to others so they don't get associated with failure. They throw another employee or department under the bus instead of owning the mistake and fixing it. As long as the failure doesn't get attributed to their name, they don't care if the problem gets fixed or not.

In a customer-focused role, the customer can quickly become an obstacle for the employee to show their value. After all, customers are unpredictable. They can be difficult to please. An insecure team member can actually feel a sense of hostility toward a customer.

On the flip side, though, a team member who feels secure and successful in their role will bend over backward to help a customer. The customer becomes yet another vehicle for the team member's success. They're an opportunity for future promotions or pay raises.

For a team member to feel secure and successful in their role, they need to perceive these things:

- I am good at my job.
- My leader is satisfied with me.

- My team members are satisfied with me.
- I am growing.
- Others succeeding doesn't mean I don't succeed.
- I get credit for my contribution.

Secure team members make the guest feel valued, but they also make other team members feel valued. Security in the team becomes a self-fulfilling prophecy of sorts.

Take a moment and examine your teams. Are they secure? Or do they shift blame, scramble to get credit, or even show indifference in their role? If they do, a culture of encouraging others is one of the ways you can turn that around. It starts with you as a leader, but it also needs to happen among the ranks.

One way to create that culture in your team is through rewarding those who celebrate others. Think of it like a crime-tips hotline, but for good things. Did someone do something great in the organization? Reward the person who brings that to your attention as well as the person who did the great thing.

Sometimes simple affirmation is enough. What gets recognized gets repeated. And when you recognize it publicly, it sets a standard for the whole team.

You could also do something more tangible like gift cards, swag items from the company, or periods of bigger discounts for products the company produces.

The point is, there need to be rewards attached to sharing credit. There need to be incentives for encouraging fellow team members. That creates a sense of hospitality on your team, and a team who cares for each other feels unified. A unified team can do amazing things for the guest.

Do you see your employees as problems? If so, they'll probably see their customers as problems. But when you see your employees as valuable and they see themselves that way, they'll love and value the customer.

Key Points and Takeaways

1. Great customer hospitality requires an element of trust among members of your company. Team members should feel supported by and unified with their managers and coworkers.

2. Your organization should have a culture of assuming the best. That will mean countering bad experiences employees have had and creating reliable opportunities for feedback to close communication gaps.

3. A certain sense of camaraderie is vital to the hospitality of a team. Great organizations create avenues of connection between their coworkers.

4. There should be no trade secrets within departments of your organization. Promote learning from and teaching others in your teams.

5. Your team members need to believe:

   a. I am good at my job.

   b. My leader is satisfied with me.

   c. My team members are satisfied with me.

   d. I am growing.

   e. Others succeeding doesn't mean I don't succeed.

   f. I get credit for my contribution.

appendix

Sample Psychographic Sheet

Rather than choose an actual business or create a fictitious business to make a psychographic sheet for, we decided to do something a little bit different. (Assuming you're reading this now, our publisher let this happen, so thanks, guys.) In the movie *Dodgeball*, there are two rival gyms: Globo Gym and Average Joe's Gymnasium.[1] There's a clear distinction between the two gyms' target clientele, so we thought we would show the differences using these gyms as the sample.

The two personas are Briana (mentioned briefly in one scene), and Gordon, played by Stephen Root. They are great personas of the types of people the two gyms reach. And by targeting everything their customer service does for those guests, the two gyms will become much more effective at creating a remarkable experience for them.

Globo Gym

Target: Briana
Age: 24
Location: Waldorf, California
Relationship status: single, actively dating
Children: none
Housing: upscale apartment in downtown area, well decorated, with a dog as her only roommate
Education: bachelor's degree in business from UCLA
Employment: upwardly mobile marketing career
Vehicle: new black BMW or Audi
Finances: affluent, plenty of discretionary income
Food: healthy snacks, smoothies, vitamin water, juices
Social life: casual friends, hanging out at trendy restaurants and bars in the evenings
Favorite magazines: *Shape, Us Weekly*
TV shows: CNBC, HGTV, *The Bachelor, The Bachelorette*
Shopping: Lululemon Athletica, J. Crew, boutique clothing stores
Social media: uses social media primarily as an influencer, also uses Tinder to find dates
Primary needs: feeling superior to others, being attractive and popular
Music: electronic dance music
Interests: primarily social interests without a lot of extra time because of a desire to climb the ladder of her company

Average Joe's Gymnasium

Target: Gordon

Age: 32

Location: Waldorf, California

Relationship status: married, unhappily

Children: two—ages seven and five

Housing: comfortable and simple house in the suburbs, built in the 1960s

Education: one semester of junior college

Employment: government job

Vehicle: used, older Toyota Corolla needing frequent maintenance

Finances: financially strained

Food: beer, pub food, pizza

Social life: small group of friends he sees primarily at work and the gym

Favorite magazines: *Obscure Sports Quarterly*, *Consumer Reports*

TV shows: ESPN8: "The Ocho," *The Big Bang Theory*, *CSI*, *Law and Order*

Shopping: Target, Walmart

Social media: primarily only for keeping up with his friends and sharing memes

Primary needs: losing a few pounds, getting healthier, and making some good friends in the process

Music: 2000s rap and R & B

Interests: weekend hobbies, largely inactive

NOTES

Chapter 2 Create a Culture, Not a Job Title

1. Anthony of Padua, *Sermons* I.226.
2. "Workplace Culture: What It Is, Why It Matters, & How to Define It," ERC, February 1, 2019, http://www.yourerc.com/blog/post/Work place-Culture-What-it-Is-Why-it-Matters-How-to-Define-It.aspx.
3. Matt Viser, "Joe Biden Unspools an Endless Supply of 'Bidenisms' on the Campaign Trail," *Washington Post*, January 24, 2020, https://www .washingtonpost.com/politics/joe-biden-unspools-an-endless-supply-of -biden-isms-on-the-campaign-trail/2020/01/24/475033b4-3eba-11ea-b90d -5652806c3b3a_story.html.

Chapter 3 Know the Guest

1. Grady McGregor, "U.S. Brands Think They Understand China's Market, but a New Report Says They Don't," *Fortune*, January 17, 2020, https:// fortune.com/2020/01/17/us-brands-china-hong-kong-lewis-research -marketing.
2. Jairo Senise, "Who Is Your Next Customer?," Strategy+Business, August 29, 2007, http://www.strategy-business.com/article/07313?_ref =http://en.wikipedia.org/wiki/Psychographi.
3. Tony Morgan is a leadership coach/consultant. He has a great article on his website from which we adapted these problem-solving questions: "Don't Blame Your Staff! 6 Steps to Fixing Broken Systems," Tony Morgan Live, September 19, 2017, tonymorganlive.com/2017/09/19/fixing -broken-church-systems.

Chapter 4 Be Fully Present

1. Gordan Peerman, *Blessed Relief: What Christians Can Learn from Buddhists about Suffering* (Woodstock, VT: SkyLight Paths, 2008), 6.
2. Eric Wargo, "How Many Seconds to a First Impression?," Association for Psychological Science, July 2006, http://www.psychologicalscience.org/index.php/publications/observer/2006/july-06/how-many-seconds-to-a-first-impression.html.

Chapter 6 Recover Quickly

1. Holly Stiel, *The Art and Science of the Hotel Concierge* (Orlando: Educational Institute, 2013), 212.
2. Proverbs 15:1.

Chapter 7 Observe Details, Because Everything Communicates

1. Joseph Michelli, *The Starbucks Experience* (New York: McGraw-Hill Education, 2006), 54.
2. Matthew May, "The Story behind the Famous FedEx Logo, and Why It Works," Co.Design newsletter, October 23, 2012, http://www.fastcodesign.com/1671067/the-story-behind-the-famous-fedex-logo-and-why-it-works.

Chapter 9 Choose Values over Policies

1. Dale Carnegie, *How to Win Friends and Influence People* (New York: First Pocket Books, 1982), 242.

Chapter 10 Build a Hospitable Team

1. Alice Truong, "How Jack Dorsey Makes Meetings at Square More Transparent," Fast Company, November 5, 2013, https://www.fastcompany.com/3021208/how-jack-dorsey-makes-meetings-at-square-transparent.
2. Blusk, "Our 3-D Scrapbook," Southwest (blog), August 16, 2006, https://community.southwest.com/t5/Blog/Our-3-D-Scrapbook/ba-p/6758.

Appendix

1. *Dodgeball*, directed by Rawson Marshall Thurber (Los Angeles: 20th Century Fox, 2004).

Jason Young is a keynote speaker, an executive coach, and a consultant. He helps organizations develop emotionally intelligent leaders, build healthy teams, and create remarkable customer experiences. He has worked with Chick-fil-A, Ford Motor Company, Gorilla Glue, FedEx, and other respected companies. Jason has an earned doctoral degree in the field of hospitality. He lives in Atlanta, Georgia. Learn more at catchfiredaily.com.

Jonathan Malm is an entrepreneur and business owner. He runs SundaySocial.tv and ChurchStageDesignIdeas.com, reaching more than 70,000 leaders each month. Jonathan consults with organizations regularly on guest services and creative expression. He lives in San Antonio, Texas.

MORE RESOURCES FROM JASON AND JONATHAN

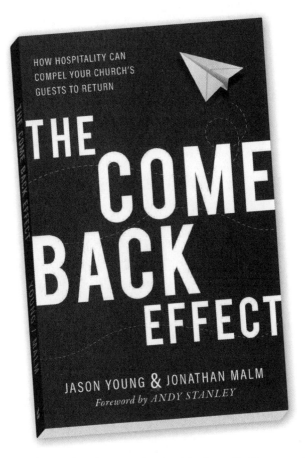

Written by a church consultant and a hospitality expert, *The Come Back Effect* shows you the secret to helping a first-time guest return again and again. Through this engaging, story-driven approach, you'll discover how to develop and implement changes that lead to repeat visits and, eventually, to sustained growth in your church or ministry.

Your most effective volunteers are already in your church!

Here's how to find—and keep—them.

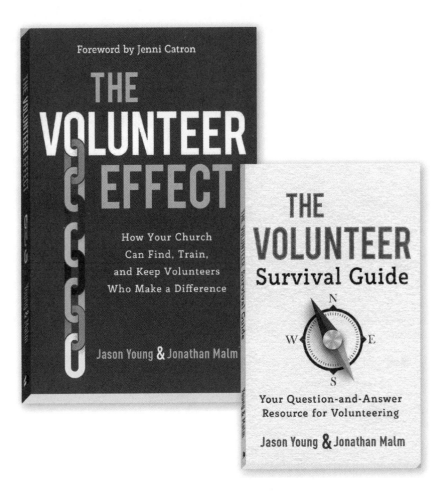

Learn how to invite, train, and retain excellent volunteers.

We help develop leaders, engage their team members, and boost brand likability with guests to ignite a healthy culture that can't be extinguished. This is Catch Fire.

Head to **catchfiredaily.com** to learn about workshops and events, download resources, listen to the *Catch Fire* podcast, read case studies, and connect with Jason.

📷	**CatchFireDaily**
f	**CatchFireDaily**
▶	**Catch Fire**
in	**CatchFireDaily**